MOORE RUBLE YUDELL
Building in Berlin

To Catdal

Happy Birthday

Cheers

John.

May 2001.

Introduction by Michael Webb
Edited by Adrian Koffka and Wendy Kohn

MOORE RUBLE YUDELL
Building in Berlin

images
Publishing

Introduction by Michael Webb
Edited by Adrian Koffka and Wendy Kohn

First published in Australia in 1999 by
The Images Publishing Group Pty Ltd
ACN 059 734 431
6 Bastow Place, Mulgrave, Victoria 3170, Australia
Telephone: (+61 3) 9561 5544 Facsimile: (+61 3) 9561 4860
Email: books@images.com.au

National Library of Australia Cataloguing-in-Publication Data

Moore Ruble Yudell: building in Berlin 1980–2000.

Bibliography.
Includes index.
ISBN 1 86470 026 2.

1. Moore, Ruble, Yudell, Architects & Planners. 2. Architecture–Germany–Berlin. 3. Architecture, Modern–20th century–Germany–Berlin. I. Moore, Ruble, Yudell, Architects & Planners.

720.943155

Edited by Stephen Dobney

Designed by The Graphic Image Studio Pty Ltd
Mulgrave, Australia

Film separations by Rainbow Graphics

Printed in Hong Kong by Paramount

Contents

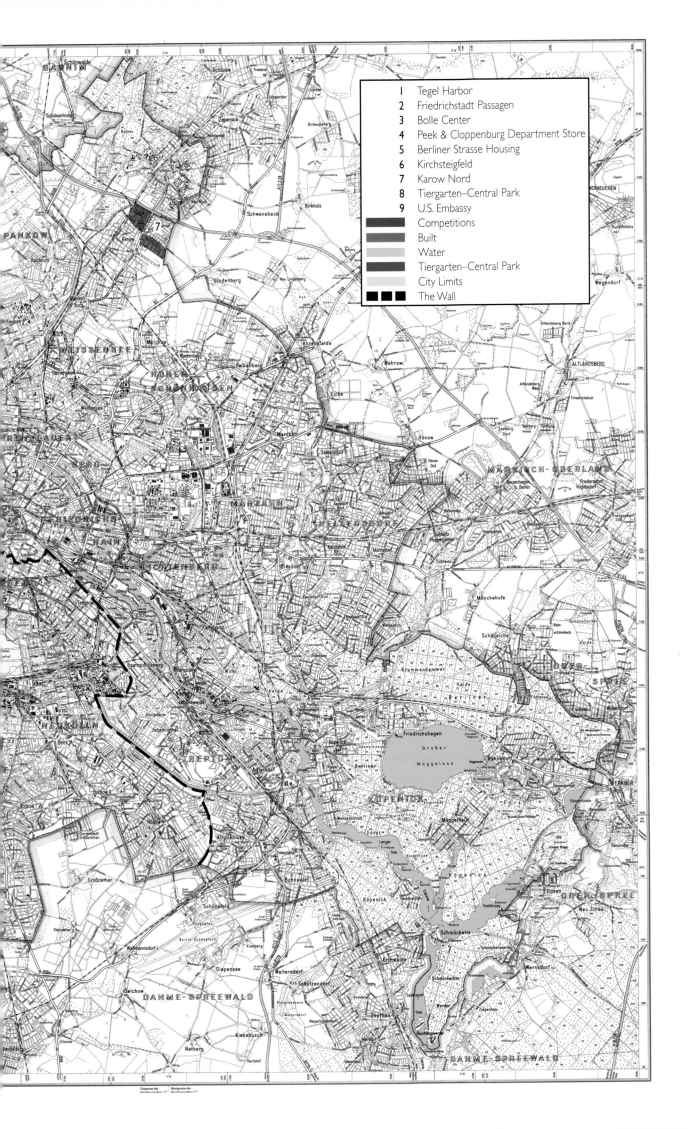

1	Tegel Harbor
2	Friedrichstadt Passagen
3	Bolle Center
4	Peek & Cloppenburg Department Store
5	Berliner Strasse Housing
6	Kirchsteigfeld
7	Karow Nord
8	Tiergarten–Central Park
9	U.S. Embassy
	Competitions
	Built
	Water
	Tiergarten–Central Park
	City Limits
	The Wall

UNDIVIDED: THE PROJECTS OF MOORE RUBLE YUDELL IN BERLIN 1980–2000

Introduction
By Michael Webb

Los Angeles—the home of Moore Ruble Yudell—and Berlin—home to much of the firm's work—are twinned cities and have much in common. Both are upstart metropolises that have undergone explosive growth over the past 130 years, attracting ambitious immigrants and stretching their boundaries to incorporate farms and small towns. The influx of talent and fusion of cultures have made each city a center of innovation. There is an underlying energy and restlessness, a sense of unlimited possibilities, that excites and alarms outsiders. Both cities have been severely tried—Berlin by the destruction of war and political division, L.A. by riots and natural disasters—and have demonstrated their resilience.

In the first half of the 20th century, the cultural flow was from Berlin to L.A., as Hollywood lured the finest artists of Weimar Germany, then welcomed refugees from Nazi oppression. In the second, the flow was reversed, as many of those émigrés returned home, and Americans participated in the rebuilding and sustenance of West Berlin. As a result of these exchanges, L.A. was the first American city to embrace European Modernism, and Berlin has had a complicated love–hate relationship with the U.S. since the 1920s.

During the three decades that the Wall divided Berlin, each half of the city was rebuilt as a showcase of competing ideologies. In the East, the Palace of the Republic, the television tower, and the rebuilt Alexanderplatz proclaimed the triumph of socialism. In the West, the Culture Forum, Free University, and the glittering stores along the Kurfürstendamm were among the trophies of democratic capitalism. Nowhere was the contrast greater than in housing. The Stalinallée was designed in grandiose Soviet style to house workers in palatial splendor, but, behind this Potemkin facade lay serried rows of precast concrete barracks. The West inherited the bourgeois suburbs, most of which were restored after the war, and the tenements of Kreuzberg, which were appropriated by young artists and radicals. The Bonn government offered varied incentives to boost settlement in this beleaguered outpost, financing unpretentious low-income apartment buildings and a few demonstration projects, notably the international building exhibitions (IBA) of 1957 and 1987.

The first IBA produced the Hansa Quarter, a centrally located complex of tower blocks, garden apartments, and landscaping created by 53 architects from 14 countries. The later project, which marked the 750th anniversary of Berlin and the shift from Modernism to Postmodernism, attracted 200 architects who competed for the privilege of planning or building on 90 scattered sites. In 1987, the goal was to stitch up the urban fabric, which had been rent by massive clearances and the Modernist fashion for object buildings. The official brief was to "pick up historical traces, respect the traditional layout, and conserve existing buildings." The chief enforcer of this policy was Josef Kleihues, then Berlin's authoritative city architect, who insisted on diversity, giving several firms a stake in the master plan for each block or neighborhood.

Each architect was to bring fresh ideas but to work within agreed limits of density, height, and layout.

One of the more controversial of the IBA projects was located near the northwestern edge of the city at Tegel, a lakeside community that is also known for its busy airport and for Schloss Humboldt, a Neoclassical country house by Karl Friedrich Schinkel. Tegel Harbor was formerly a coal port, supplied by boat through a network of waterways, and a vital supply depot during the 1949 Berlin Airlift. In 1974, one hundred German architects submitted proposals for its redevelopment, but the municipal council of Reinickendorf was dissatisfied with the results and withheld its approval. As the concept for IBA took shape, the Berlin planning director, who lived in the area, persuaded Kleihues to add this fringe site to his roster. Charles Moore, then at the height of his fame, was invited to compete, alongside Ralph Erskine (Sweden), Arata Isozaki (Japan), and Rob Krier (Luxembourg). Moore developed his master plan with the Moore Ruble Yudell (MRY) office in Los Angeles, and they won the 1980 competition with a complex of 320 housing units (sandwiched between the harbor and Tegel village), a swim stadium on an island, and a cultural complex at the tip of the inlet. The scheme wove together landscaping and buildings of varied heights in a loose yet coherent composition, stepping down from the existing tower blocks at the end of the site to the modest scale of the village.

Werner Weber, who was then planning officer for Reinickendorf and a member of the local IBA jury, remembers that he and his municipal colleagues "fought for the MRY design because it brought water close to the town, because the heights were moderate, and because there was a good balance between residential, cultural, and commercial components which could be built separately as funding became available. The scheme was people-friendly and it strengthened the center of the borough." The potential for phased development proved critical. The city authorities provided DM 20 million to enlarge the harbor, construct a waterfront promenade, and strengthen the banks of the island. However, plans for a graduate music school, a performance space, an art rental library, and a stadium were all deferred, and the only cultural element to be built was the Humboldt Library.

A year after the first phase was completed, the Berlin Wall came down; the city and private firms were overwhelmed by competing opportunities, and the expansion of Tegel was shelved. Only now has a developer begun to consider an alternative scheme of housing for seniors on the forested island, and a trio of plazas that would step up from the edge of the housing to the library, finally uniting it with the rest of Tegel Harbor.

Moore Ruble Yudell's competition-winning master plan shows three mid-rise blocks separated by wide swathes of landscaping from the serpentine row houses. In the final version, the components have been pulled together in a tight-knit urban complex. Four four-story blocks linked by four gateways define an octagonal courtyard. An axial footpath runs through this courtyard into the commons—partly enclosed by a curving range of seven six-story blocks—and out through another gate to the waterfront promenade.[1] The plan achieves a balance between the openness and informality of southern California and the romantic German tradition of buildings framed by landscape that is exemplified by Schloss Humboldt.

Responsibility for the design of the housing was shared between MRY, who spent two years refining its competition entry, five international stars, and local architects who emerged from the firm of Jonzen Schultze

I

2

3

Weber Steinebach (winner of the 1974 contest) who got to build the undulating ranges of four-story row houses that separate the villas along the south boundary from the MRY blocks to the north. The villas were designed by MRY, Antoine Grumbach, John Hejduk with Moritz Muller, Paolo Portoghesi, Robert Stern, and Stanley Tigerman, Fugman, McCurry. The strength and elasticity of the plan comfortably accommodates this concentration of architectural egos and lively self-expression.

The MRY apartment blocks are monumental yet playful, their mass broken up by balconies and dormer windows, which add space and variety to the small living units. Mock rustication, cornices, and arches evoke a classical order in the facades, and these devices are enhanced by the palette of pale grays and warm pastels that was designed by Tina Beebe.[2] Zinc roofs gleam in the pale northern light. Scale, tonality, and language owe a debt to Schinkel, but the buildings also incorporate a strong element of fantasy. At the center of the main block, on axis, a cluster of gables rise to suggest a tower, which is topped by two chimneys and an arch. Devices like these angered purists, who dismissed MRY's designs as "Disneyesque," but the public

response was generally favorable, and these tiny apartments have been eagerly sought-after.

The success of Tegel Harbor has much to do with the way it fits into its pastoral setting; most residents are delighted that the swim stadium was not built, leaving the island as a tranquil green refuge. Handsome iron rails border the serpentine promenade, which is shaded by maples and linden trees, and the bridges to the island. Over the past ten years, the landscaping has matured and filled out what was originally a bare site, thanks to the creativity of Cornelia Müller, Jan Wehberg, and their former associate, Elmar Knippschild.[3] This landscape architecture firm was established only a year before the Tegel competition, and its young principals remember their excitement in meeting Charles Moore and John Ruble just after they had won. Müller boldly pleaded for the elimination of the carports, and she worked with MRY to put parking underground and conceal the access ramps. That required an added layer of earth to sustain grass and hedges, and strategically located pits for trees. Elaborate planting diagrams gave way to naturalistic designs that incorporated an existing row of poplars along the waterfront.

Wehberg complains that the landscaping has become too exuberant—that the ivy covering the inner walls of the courtyard should be cut back and the trees pruned and culled to maintain a good balance between greenery and buildings.

The Humboldt Library was inspired by the industrial lofts that once occupied the site, but that was just a point of departure for the plain but dignified facade, with its cut-away barrel vault, Palladian end windows, and symbolic entry arch (echoing the arch that frames the recessed entrance of the MRY villa). Stucco columns frame expansive windows down the sides, and a glazed slot set into the vault pulls natural light into the heart of the building on Berlin's frequent dull days. Today, the handsome exterior is marred by graffiti; ironically the Germans, who make such a fetish of order and cleanliness, seem entirely indifferent to this ubiquitous vandalism, perhaps mistaking it for artistic expression. In that respect, "the Wall"—where protest was appropriate—set a dangerous precedent.

4

The care for the library's interior makes up for the neglect of the facade. It is a glorious, soaring hall, divided asymmetrically by a row of concrete and steel columns supporting an inner vault of wood slats that echoes the bowed outer vault with its ribbed-metal lining. A mezzanine gallery loops around the circular reception desk and slices across the hall, linking the upstairs reading room (the children's library is tucked in beneath) with a wedge of book stacks. Witty cut-outs of perforated metal form a screen of arches that leads to mock pediments atop the stacks. Structure and ornament, orthogonal geometries and sensual curves, the warm embrace of wood and the cool shimmer of aluminum are all in perfect balance. The space is layered and kinetic and turns everyday routine into a joyful adventure.

Tegel and its library represented the last flourish of extravagance in Berlin, for it was planned and built at a time when no price seemed too high to uphold this fortress of freedom.[4] A year after the Wall came down and the city was reunited, it became clear that the authorities could no longer afford IBA-type projects. The euphoria that had greeted reunification dissipated. The German economy was strained by recession and the awesome cost of bailing out the moribund provinces of the former DDR. Huge investments were being made to transform the desolate juncture of East and West into a vibrant hub for multinational corporations.

The exuberance of Tegel sparked controversy among committed Modernists, but its popular success opened many doors. MRY made an impressive showing in competitions for three commercial structures, although its entries did not have the success they deserved. The Bolle Center, a mixed-use complex, took its cues from the adjoining Spree Canal, fanning out low-rise wings and public gardens. Three commercial–residential blocks on the Friedrichstrasse were to be linked by a shopping passage that would restore the pre-war fame of this street. The design for the Peek & Cloppenburg clothing store on the fashionable Tauentzienstrasse ranged the shopping floors around a glass atrium; although an alternative design was chosen, MRY was asked to build a similar store in Leipzig.

Dieter Graalfs, one of the partners in the Berlin development company Groth + Graalfs, commissioned the firm to design Berlinerstrasse, a group of villas that would contain 75 luxury apartments on a lakeside site near the Glienecke Bridge of Cold War fame. Soon after, he invited MRY to submit their ideas for Kirchsteigfeld, a mixed-use community of 10,000 that his company would build and maintain on the southeast edge of

Potsdam in the former DDR. The site was a 53-hectare wedge of farmland bordered by an autobahn, the medieval hamlet of Drewitz, and an oak-lined allée, with an estate of DDR slab blocks beyond.

Kirchsteigfeld was conceived and built with great care and astonishing rapidity. Groth + Graalfs signed an urban development contract with the local authorities, establishing a public–private partnership that worked to the advantage of all, and Graalfs forged a personal alliance with Richard Rohrbein, the director of city planning for Potsdam. Six architects, including MRY and Rob Krier, were invited to participate in an interactive workshop, debating their respective plans for the new community. As Ruble recalls: "Rob had drawn beautiful plans of an almost medieval town: narrow, crooked streets, formed by small closed residential blocks leading to shaped squares with a powerful figure–ground composition."

In contrast, the MRY plan was airy, proposing a modified grid of straight streets lined by generously scaled blocks that were open to the street and built around landscaped courtyards. There was a strong but permeable boundary line, and the plan incorporated two natural features: the allée along the north side and the Hintergraben, an irrigation canal that bisects the site from east to west, neither of which appears on Krier's original plan. The MRY plan had a pleasing simplicity that drew on the firm's designs for Playa Vista, a community of similar scale on the edge of Los Angeles that was strongly influenced by the New Urbanism of Duany/Plater-Zyberk, another member of the L.A. planning team. It also drew on the enlightened plans of the Berlin Siedlungen—model housing estates of the 1920s that were designed by such architects as Hugo Haring and Bruno Taut.

Graalfs indicated his strong preference for the MRY approach, but a second workshop had been scheduled, and Krier, with his partner Christoph Kohl, radically revised his plans, opening up the streets and the blocks and incorporating the best features of his rival's design. Graalfs had worked with Krier on an IBA project in Berlin in the mid 1980s and now decided that he should do the master plan of Kirchsteigfeld, sharing responsibility for the architecture with the five workshop participants and 16 other architects, ranging from the London offices of Skidmore, Owings & Merrill, and Kohn Pedersen Fox to the fledgling Berlin practice of Lunetto & Fischer.

There were to be 2,200 subsidized apartments, 600 condominiums and row houses, a main square with a church at its center, and two tree-lined axes that bypass the square. One is the main north–south road; the other is the waterway which leads to a pond, both of which are augmented by rainwater which must, according to German law, remain on site. Because of the high water table, there are no service basements; as a result, storage sheds and carports with landscaped roofs block off the ground stories of most blocks. Krier would have preferred to give over entire blocks to a single architect, but Graalfs insisted that, to achieve variety, each component building be designed by a different firm. MRY designed 25, of which 15 were built. However, Krier enforced strict guidelines, as did the color consultant, Werner Spillmann, so that every designer worked within tight constraints and was given limited opportunity for self-expression.

The product of this somewhat authoritarian approach is controlled and controlling. For all the efforts to mandate variety through varied forms and heights (generally five stories at street corners and four in between), the town was clearly realized as a whole and lacks the elements of surprise and serendipity that characterize piecemeal growth. Krier would argue that Potsdam itself—and a hundred other vibrant communities, from Versailles to Siena—were planned with similar rigor and have adapted well to changing patterns of use. Part of the problem at Kirchsteigfeld is its rawness, which will diminish as the strident colors fade and the trees fill out. Another is the blandness in much of the architecture: the budget for subsidized housing is limited, and refinements such as rooftop loggias were eliminated.

The major difficulty may lie in Krier's wholesale rejection of Modernism and his insistence on a Platonic ideal of town-making—an approach that can easily turn sterile, as it did in Renaissance planned towns like Palmanova when intellect overwhelmed intuition. Some early Modern estates may have been too diagrammatic, but they brought light, air, and green open space to workers formerly confined to tenements, and the best of them—like Onkel-Toms-Hutt—are architecturally impressive. Kirchsteigfeld has many pretty vistas and the landscaping (by Müller & Wehberg) is inspired, but there's an air of unreality about the place, as though one had strayed onto the movie set of a model town—as The Truman Show portrayed Seaside

5

in Florida. Though Krier's plan was opened up, the buildings feel too high for the narrow streets and modest circles, giving one a sense of being trapped in a maze. MRY made a valuable contribution to the project but would probably have generated a far richer and more relaxed complex if they had been put in charge.[5] However, given the choices of affordable housing in the former DDR, Kirchsteigfeld must seem like paradise to its new residents, and they have participated enthusiastically in neighborhood activities, creating a viable social entity within a year of moving in.

Groth + Graalfs, which was established in Berlin in 1982, decided to stay put after the Wall fell, and found abundant opportunities within and around the city to be enlightened patrons of architecture and socially responsible developers. People began offering them much larger sites than they had been able to acquire in the western enclave. Kirchsteigfeld was first; soon after they purchased 98 hectares of farmland adjoining the village of Karow, just inside the northeastern boundary of Berlin. They applied for permission to build there in 1992, just as the authorities were projecting demand from immigrants for 90,000 housing units over the next five years. Twenty-seven new housing developments, including the one proposed by Groth + Graalfs, were approved by the Senate, and the agricultural zoning was changed to permit mixed-use construction.

Like Kirchsteigfeld, Karow Nord was to be a public–private partnership, but with many more participants and much unnecessary conflict. Dr. Hans Stimmann, the housing czar of Berlin, had outspoken views on the kind of development he wanted. Like Krier, he felt that Le Corbusier and his followers had destroyed the traditional European city; however, he wanted to return, not to the Classical era, but to 1914, using the old neighborhoods of Berlin and English garden cities as models. Karow was to be a Vorstadt— a satellite town with a strong character. "The Siedlungen are too uniform: they were built for industrial workers and their families—a sector of society that has largely vanished in the West," says Stimmann. "Today, half the occupants are single. As city building director, you are responsible for hundreds of thousands of people and, if you are honest, you have to acknowledge what's gone wrong. People forget the wisdom of old ways, and it's a characteristic of Berlin to repudiate history."

Graalfs proposed MRY for the master plan, but Stimmann disliked the Postmodern vocabulary of Tegel and objected to the choice, even before agreeing that he and the developer would each pick three firms and jointly select a seventh and that all should compete for the plan. Both men were concerned to define the ground rules. They established a target of 5,000 units, 4,500 of which would be rented. Both insisted on modestly scaled buildings with pitched tiled roofs, considering them friendlier and because the attics would provide bonus space to supplement the modest living areas mandated by the subsidy program. They wanted Karow Nord to have a high quality of life and make a clean break with the monotonous prefabricated slabs that were favored by the DDR. The battle of the roofs—flat versus pitched—was first fought by Modernists and traditionalists in Weimar-era Berlin. Now the issue has acquired an ideological overlay, for the Nazis characterized the flat roofs and rational construction of the Bauhaus as "cultural Bolshevism," and demanded a volkische character in housing and a ponderous Classicism for their public buildings. As a result, these styles have been tainted by association, and Stimmann recalls how two young architects refused to compromise on this matter and rejected the opportunity to build in Karow. MRY would have preferred a mix of flat and pitched roofs with a choice of facing materials but, lacking a strong political conviction, went along with the requirement.

Stimmann's office organized the competition, which began with a lively four-day workshop. As Miller Stevens, a young planner who witnessed the debate and later played an important role in shaping Karow Nord, recalls: "The Berlin architects were very stubborn and inflexible, proposing repetitive layouts of standard units. In contrast, MRY understood that this was not an object from space plunked down in the city, but an opportunity to build on what was there. Their plan varied the grid to accommodate different building types and tried to embed it in its context. John and Buzz tried to find the right way by asking questions rather than staking out positions."

MRY won the competition for the Karow Nord plan, with a design for two of the four sectors that were being considered for development. There was some resistance to the idea of an American firm assuming such a challenging responsibility. As Daniel Garness, who became project director for MRY, soon discovered: "Berliners feel that they alone

understand how to build in the city. We had planned to go over there from L.A. every month or even open an office in Berlin to develop the B-Plan, a minutely detailed set of specifications required to bring the design into conformity with German planning law. However, it was suggested we turn the job over to a representative group and review what they were doing, and we did bring in a German firm to work on the plan. But we soon discovered that they couldn't grasp the layering of urban typologies, the articulation of space, and our strong interest in making it contextual. I learned how the process worked and saw that they were mashing it to pulp. Luckily, we enlisted Miller Stevens to help us with the plan, and he brought in Eva Lunetto and Jörg Fischer as associate architects. Miller and I would talk daily and I would go over for a week at a time, but this preliminary stage stretched out to 12 months, and we had to fight all that time to keep the complexities."

The planning process became even more confused when Groth + Graalfs sold off a third of the site to two other companies and each of the three retained six or seven architects to design individual buildings within its sectors. Stimmann's staff, the Berlin city planner, and a host of city and local bureaucrats became involved in the negotiations. Stevens recalls one meeting that was attended by 35 architects from the participating firms. Stimmann told them what could and could not be done, and the reaction was one of amazement, since none had anticipated such restrictive guidelines.

The justification for employing 20 firms for the three sites under Moore Ruble Yudell's master-planning direction was to foster variety and give an opportunity to small offices that lacked the staff to handle a large volume of work. It was a recipe that worked fairly well at Kirchsteigfeld, where authority was concentrated in the hands of Krier, but at Karow Nord it generated confusion. Inexperienced architects felt they were being put into straitjackets and asked to dance; understandably, many felt frustrated or resentful, and turned in mediocre designs. As Garness noted: "Few understood the importance of creating diversity within a context, and working with the constraints to do beautiful things. Their interest was in creating stand-alone object buildings, not collaborating on a larger entity." One bold attempt to vary conventional forms with boat-shaped roofs was criticized as inappropriate, though it was eventually built. Tina Beebe devised a palette of colors and

discovered that many local architects were indifferent about the choices they were asked to make.

Graalfs, whose vision Karow Nord had been, left the company, and Stimmann delegated key decisions to his staff. Bureaucrats from the former DDR were sometimes on a different wavelength from their Western-trained colleagues. City and developers wanted to axe costs. At times, the MRY team felt as though it was fighting in the trenches, but the troops toughed it out and achieved many of their goals. After two years, Karow Nord began to take shape, and early responses were enthusiastic. "We heard that it was getting a tremendous press and was being touted as a model," recalls Garness. "We won the battle for the plan and didn't lose anything of importance in the urban spaces. The distribution of density, the way it is integrated into the landscape and evokes the linear grain of the fields: those are the things that matter." Stevens concurs: "We had to work 8-day weeks and 30-hour days. You've got to put love, blood and sweat into a project to make it good and enduring."

In contrast to the compact wedge of Kirchsteigfeld, the Karow Nord site comprises two distinct plots that are separated by a main

6

7

road and linked by a narrow commercial strip, which is lined by a market, small shops, and offices. These proved difficult to rent in the midst of the recession, and the developers made compromises in the design to lure prospective tenants.[6] Stimmann persuaded the educational authority to adopt a linear plan for the high school, and this strengthens the line of the major cross road. However, the eight kindergartens, which were the subject of separate competitions, are as undistinguished as the commercial buildings, and these red brick markers have less impact on the townscape than MRY intended. Some of the rental blocks and the townhouses for which the developers assumed responsibility are mediocre. But, in most parts of the town, the quality of the whole is greater than the sum of the parts.

The varied sizes of units within each building ensures a good mix of ages and incomes, with retirees living next to young families and socializing in the spacious stair halls. Each tiny apartment has a balcony, terrace, or corner patio. Building heights and the pitch of the roofs are varied throughout. Five-story courtyard blocks have corner entrances, with paths running through diagonally. Paved

parking areas open off the street—only the townhouses have lock-up garages—and this ensures a lively mix of activities.

Planning, building, and landscape combine most successfully in the Karow court sector.[7] MRY decided to relate the new town to the old by adapting the local vernacular of varied buildings enclosing a courtyard, but opening them up at several points to create hierarchies of public and private spaces. One enters the landscaped courtyards from gently curving, tree-lined streets and walks through to the commons. An elaborate series of culverts and buried pipes channels rainwater to a deep pool that is naturally sealed by a stratum of clay. The pool enhances the landscape and serves as an emergency flood basin, but Müller and Wehberg had to fight for a year to give it an irregular shape after the bureaucrats insisted it be square! They also stretched a meager budget to create other green spaces, garden pavilions, and a variety of plantings.

Karow Nord was built at great speed, despite the impediments and the tight budget, yet it already feels lived-in. Graalfs regrets what was sacrificed but is justly proud of what was achieved against the odds. "It's wonderful to create an environment that will enrich the lives of the residents and the children growing up there," he says. "Architects often forget for whom they create their buildings. MRY knew what would work—and they succeeded. People love it."

MRY recently designed a house for Dieter Graalfs and accepted a commission from his former company to contribute two blocks— one of apartments, the other of offices—to Tiergarten Dreieck, a prestigious mixed-use development on a triangular site bordering Berlin's most famous park. In addition to the offices and housing, the project includes a new headquarters building for the Christian Democrats, embassies for Mexico and Yemen, and a third for all five Scandinavian countries, which have combined their resources to build six glass cubes surrounded by an undulating copper wall. These blocks enclose a sunken pocket park that the public can access from the street.

Each of MRY's Berlin projects has marked an important moment in the history of the city. Tegel Harbor proclaimed humane values at the periphery of the West just before the barriers fell. Berlinerstrasse was intended to reclaim a site that symbolized German civilization and natural beauty before it was brutalized. The three commercial projects reflected the optimistic assumptions of the newly reunited city. Kirchsteigfeld and Karow Nord brought an improved standard of living to East Germany, welcoming it back into the fold after 60 years of oppression. Tiergarten Dreieck, with its three embassies and CDU HQ, is a major addition to Berlin as the capital of a reunited Germany. Each of these projects has a strong sense of place, developed in response to context, and creating something fresh.

The culmination of this two-decade engagement with Berlin will be the new U.S. Embassy, located on its original pre-war site in the southwest corner of the Pariser Platz, close to the Brandenburg Gate. The square was devastated by war and obliterated by the Wall; its recovery is a symbol of reunification. In 1995, MRY working with Gruen Associates was invited to compete against five other American design teams and won the commission. This was the first competition for a U.S. embassy in 40 years, since a jury gave the award to Eero Saarinen for the building in London's Grosvenor Square. However, the MRY design promises to be a far more welcome addition to the cityscape than the ponderous facade and giant bronze eagle of that earlier competition winner.

8

9

The new embassy faces north to the Pariser Platz, west to the Tiergarten, and south to the Holocaust Memorial that is to be built to the designs of another American team, architect Peter Eisenmann and artist Richard Serra. Each facade satisfies the demanding requirements of security and the Berlin building code and employs varied forms, materials, and textures to establish a lively dialogue with its neighbors. The openness of American society is symbolized by the ceremonial north entrance, where the walls part to allow sun to penetrate to the inner courtyard, revealing a rotunda.[8] A copper and glass lantern at the southwest corner lights the ambassador's stateroom and serves as an illuminated beacon at night, playing off the quadriga atop the Brandenburg Gate. From the gently curved glass canopy over the main entrance, to the south loggia that marks the consular entrance, to the roof garden that focuses on the Gate, the embassy provides public expression of unity in diversity. This theme is developed within the block, with a house-like social center that symbolizes American tradition set at the center of a landscaped courtyard. The embassy is also a model of sustainability, flexibility, and optimum working conditions.

The State Department kept the competition-winning design under wraps for nine months in deference to congressional opponents of public spending, and then demanded that the Berlin authorities reroute traffic into the Tiergarten to improve security before construction begins.[9] This issue must be resolved. It is unthinkable that the U.S. should give up its place at the center of the city it struggled to defend for more than 40 years, or to fortify what must appear to be a symbol of democracy and outreach. As ambassador Charles Redman declared: "This is the best site in the most important city of a country that is a crucial strategic ally."

For MRY, the project represents a drawing together of the threads that run through its earlier work. The embassy is an office and a symbol, a community and a place to foster relationships with leaders and the general public. It addresses the city and repairs a rent in its fabric. If built as designed, it will celebrate our country's values and be a worthy marker of the contribution MRY has made to its second home.

TEGEL HARBOR

Bird's eye view of revised competition scheme

The master plan for Tegel Harbor connects a suburban village with a chain of lakes, canals, and forested open space. The program of this international competition, which MRY won in 1980, called for residential, cultural, and sports recreation uses, with the aim of providing Berliners with a destination for weekend outings seemingly far from the city center. In response to planning guidelines, each of three major program components appears as a discrete complex on the 40-acre site.

To enhance the harbor as a strong element in the plan, the water is dramatically extended into the site. Along the water's edge, a promenade connects all three complexes with the lake beyond.

At the focus of this new waterfront, the recreation center takes the form of a small island (or a great river boat) containing an indoor/outdoor landscape of heated pools, waterfalls, beaches, and gardens. One reaches this stationary vessel by bridges and smaller boats.

Tegel Housing

This 170-unit housing complex forms part of the multi-use master plan for Tegel Harbor. An additional 150 units, designed by a variety of different architects, constitute the second phase of construction.

The housing area is intended to create a rich and varied set of connections between Tegel Village and the small harbor, whose expansion and conversion to recreational use are part of the master plan. The housing begins with a series of bright villas embraced by a second layer of gently undulating row houses. Within the row house sequence, the project establishes a courtyard with four "houses" and four gates. The axis of this court proceeds directly through two of the gates to the landscaped commons beyond, ending with a view of the harbor. This visual axis to the water is complemented by a meandering path lined

with tall poplars. In the great commons, the houses step up from five to eight stories, plus a high, zinc-covered roof. The roof itself, a lively village of dormer windows and loggias, is set upon a more ordered base of stucco walls with precast pilasters and moldings.

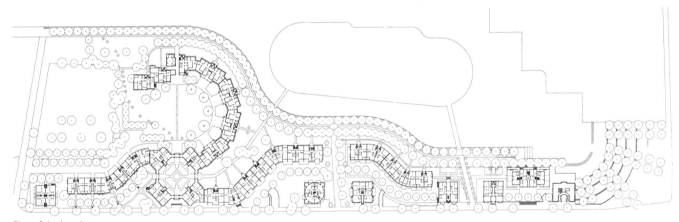

Plan of the housing

Elevation of the housing

Elevation of the housing

The social housing units are tiny, by code, but are relieved by generous loggias. Typical units afford views to both the commons—to the south—and the harbor—generally north—from their combined living/dining rooms.

The design seeks to achieve an extraordinary degree of variety within a precast concrete construction system, treating this high-density social "townhousing" as both urbane and playful.

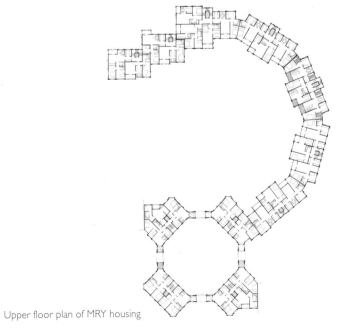

Upper floor plan of MRY housing

Villa by MRY

On the shore opposite, curved and straight rows of houses gently line the promenade, forming a series of broad landscaped or narrow paved edges to the waterfront. At the west edge of the site, the row housing steps up to form a tower, identifying the new development from more distant viewpoints.

At the northwest edge of the site lies the cultural center, with a broad sweep of steps and a tower that continue the urban character of Karolinenstrasse. The cultural center also has its own waterfront entrance leading up to the plaza, on which are placed a set of simple, almost industrial buildings. Elsewhere in Tegel, the presence of industrial structures contrasts with well-preserved buildings in a range of 19th century styles. Here, various small institutions—a library, an art gallery, a theater, and a school with well-ordered plans and classical elevations—create the feeling of waterfront warehouses.

The three complexes and the water come together at the entrance to the site, where radial rows of trees draw the visitor down to the new harbor. The harbor expansion and public promenade, along with the first phase of housing, were completed in 1987.

Tegel villas by MRY, Steinebach+Weber, Robert Stern, Stanley Tigerman

Canal between island and promenade

Following pages: Humboldt Library from the promenade

Humboldt Library

This branch library forms the first phase of the cultural center for the Tegel Harbor Master Plan. Started in 1986, its construction coincided with the creation of a large water area adjacent to the harbor, a waterfront promenade, and 350 units of housing. The library forms one edge of the cultural center, its long hall continuing the axis of the harbor along the north boundary of the site.

The industrial loft became the prototype for Humboldt Library. Its classical facade is broken by a glassy entrance bay framed by a pair of freestanding portals. This leads to a central rotunda encircled by an arcaded balcony at the second floor. From the rotunda, a grand wall of books meanders along one side of the main reading room and gives access to

Main entrance

Opposite: Foyer with information desk

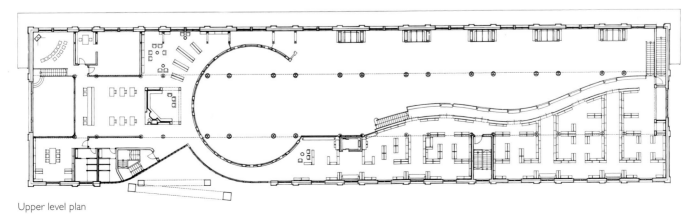

Upper level plan

Vaulted ceiling lit by clerestory window

the open stacks and smaller reading alcoves beyond. Passing continuously above the various areas of the loft is a double-layer vaulted ceiling lit by a clerestory window, which bounces light around and through the lower vault. On the north side, the light is balanced by a series of bay windows and doors that alternate with niches for books. The view from the main reading room is directed out toward a forested landscape.

Upper level balcony

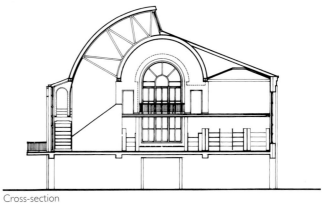

Cross-section

The steel and concrete frame is exposed on the interior; its industrial toughness is then elaborated into a playful, almost baroque set of details for arches and ceiling. The book wall itself is, like furniture, composed of painted and natural hardwood. Exterior materials—metal sash, stucco, and the standing seam zinc roof—combine with spare classical elements of precast concrete.

Book niche along north wall

Exterior facing north

Opposite: Upper level wall of books

Following pages: Library from Old Tegel center

TEGEL HARBOR

Opposite: View from library across island
to housing

A City Undivided

by Adrian Koffka

1

2

3

Charles Moore, in winning the competition for Tegel Harbor in 1980, arrived in Berlin at a time when a unified Germany seemed, at best, many generations away. The division of the country had been accepted as the result of a catastrophic era, at the end of which stood the breaking up of the world into two parts: the West and the East. Germany, then the epicenter of the catastrophe, became the border of this division. As the decades passed, peaceful change seemed unimaginable; yet another war, impossible to survive. That Berlin—East and West—was able to exist, and even flourish, during the nearly half century of German division testifies as much to its resilience as to the idiosyncrasies of history.

Founded in the early 13th century, Berlin first gained importance in the 18th century as the seat of the enlightened military kings of Prussia. This was a time when the arts were considered vital to the identity of a nation. Large-scale planning brought the city its gridded quarters, Neoclassicist landmarks, planned landscapes, and pleasure palaces.[1]

When Germany was first unified under Prussian rule in 1871, at the dusk of Absolutism and the dawn of the Industrial Age, it became the capital of an empire reaching from the North and Baltic Seas to the Alps. To accommodate legions of workers, the new urban quarters that emerged comprised tightly packed apartment blocks (as elsewhere in Europe) with few amenities, poor hygiene, and the infamous "Hinterhöfe"—back yards so narrow that sunlight could not reach the ground.[2]

Following Germany's defeat in the First World War, the German sovereigns—Emperor and all—resigned. On that day in 1918, when Karl Liebknecht pronounced a socialist republic and Kurt Scheidemann a democratic one, the philosophies of East and West clashed for the first time. While Berlin erupted into civil war, a constitutional assembly met in Weimar, where Germany's first democracy prevailed. Two years later, parliament passed the Act of Greater Berlin, which incorporated the region around the fledgling city. This periphery, a string of romantic landscapes, palace gardens, lakes and rivers, and rural communities, remains to this day a distinct and vital part of Berlin.[3]

Parallel to the growth of the worker movements and the birth of Marxist ideology, architects and city planners in the 1920s

4

5

6

began to address the poor housing conditions. With the founding of the Bauhaus, large-scale projects (the so-called "settlements") with thousands of units of housing were developed with modern amenities, access to light, and green open space. Some were company towns, others public–private partnerships, and a few, like the Gehag-Siedlungen, were run like private companies with entirely public funds.[4] Architects such as Bruno Taut and Walter Gropius tested both their architectural and social concepts, and Mies van der Rohe drafted his revolutionary ideas for a skyscraper wrapped entirely in glass—equally a symbol of the rise of technology and of a more open society.

But democracy at that time in Germany proved a short-lived experiment. Doomed by the division of parliament into extremist splinter parties, the country experienced increasing anarchy and political murder, a swiftly failing economy, and record levels of unemployment. Adolf Hitler's National Socialist Party, with its law-and-order approach, found an eager breeding ground. Hitler was elected chancellor on January 30, 1933.

The culture of Berlin was "equalized": all diversity and criticism shattered. German intellectuals, among them the architects of the Bauhaus, left in masses. But it was the Jewish community that suffered the most.

Jews had been an integral part of German society for many centuries. During the empire and first republic, Jewish Germans had risen to the highest ranks in Berlin's institutions as politicians, bankers, patrons of the arts, and artists in all fields. Max Liebermann became the most popular painter of portraits, and his palatial house on Pariser Platz, directly adjacent to the Brandenburg Gate, was one of the centers of cultural life in Berlin. While Liebermann lived to witness the rise of the Nazis, he was fortunate to pass away in his own home before the entire Jewish community was destroyed, the vast majority of its members murdered in the Holocaust. In Berlin, the Nazis masterminded this cruel genocide, and robbed the city and the continent of a culture vital to its identity.[5,6]

While the Liebermann house was rebuilt after unification as a tribute to the artist, the planned Holocaust Memorial—just a few hundred yards to the south, across the street from the U.S. Embassy site—remains on the drawing boards. After two competitions and much public debate, the people of Berlin are still divided over how to commemorate an unthinkable crime they committed against their own.

Hitler had envisioned Berlin as the glorious capital of a subjected world. In his madness, even while the country was at war, he ordered the demolition of whole city blocks to make way for his monumental plans. But apart from these destructions, his designs were never carried out, and at the end of the war with Germany in ruins, Berlin was divided. The Soviet sector covered the eastern half of the city, but also included the whole historic core, rich with treasures of art and architecture, all the way to its western portal, the Brandenburg Gate. The sickle-shaped western remainder was divided among the Americans, British, and French. The periphery was split from the city and became part of the Soviet-controlled part of the country. [7]

What was meant to be a temporary solution until a peace treaty could be negotiated was made permanent in 1949 when the Soviet-occupied sector declared the German Democratic Republic a communist state. Against the allied contract, Berlin's east sector

7

8

9

was made the new country's capital. Shortly thereafter, West Germany declared the Federal Republic and set up shop in Bonn, then a small town near the French border. [8,9] Should the country reunify, the federal constitution provided, Berlin would be restored as its capital.

In response to living on a small island surrounded by "enemy territory," the people of West Berlin developed an attitude of defiance. This place, once at the center of history, was really no longer part of any greater order. Not having much to believe in, West Berlin's citizens were left with an inherent sense of pessimism, but an unprecedented freedom of thought and expression, as well. West Berlin became a place at once involved with itself and open to the world.

In his introductory essay to this book, Michael Webb vividly describes how IBA, the international building exhibition, was part of this period. A child of the no-strings-attached subsidies that flowed into this western outpost, the exhibition was an attempt to create identity in a fractured place. For Moore Ruble Yudell, it was the beginning of an identity in Berlin, as well as in world architecture.

With its fresh and undogmatic approach, MRY's Tegel Harbor project became one of the most talked-about products of IBA, among fans and critics alike. While Moore Ruble Yudell's design draws from the precedents of Berlin's most glorious architectural periods, it constitutes no mockery of the past, but employs archetypal language in the service of an inherently modern concept of society. The villa housing type, once the prerogative of the wealthy, become small apartment buildings at Tegel, providing low-income tenants with multiple sunny exposures and a strong identity of home.[10] The library, with its rigorously Classicist appearance becomes a playful public place inside. And the artificial island, a memory of the romantic landscapes of the royal gardens, becomes a thoroughly plebeian place, complete with a public swimming pool.

For Moore Ruble Yudell, Tegel Harbor's success resulted in several commissions in other countries. For the city of Berlin, the period directly following the project's completion in the late 1980s was to constitute yet another fundamental paradigm shift. Under Gorbachev's leadership, the Soviet Union loosened its grip on its eastern European satellite states, and with little warning, one by one they shook off their handcuffs and—peacefully for the most part—renounced their totalitarian governments. Over the course of only several months, the unimaginable happened: with little fanfare, the whole world order was turned upside down, and the Cold War was over.

East Germans struggled to come to terms with their new freedom, as their homeland had immediately transitioned from Hitler's dictatorship to Soviet rule. While the common sentiments were insecurity and apprehension, there was also excitement over the possibilities: East Germans had coped for almost fifty years and now they were eager, in a world without obstacles, to test where their resilience could lead.

West Germany, meanwhile, considered unification a done deal. While the West German government carefully coordinated its steps with its European neighbors, who were uncomfortable at the thought of a newly strong Germany, it offered little to the eastern republic beyond an ultimatum for unification, laced with the implicit promise of ultimate prosperity.

10

In fact, the western elite was no longer so sure that Berlin should become the country's capital. The Federal Republic was rooted in its alliance with western Europe, after all, and moving to Berlin seemed foremost a concession to the east. Second, the members of parliament had gotten so used to sleepy Bonn that they could hardly imagine moving to a place as bustling with political controversy as Berlin. In a historic speech, former chancellor Willy Brandt reminded the parliament of its responsibility to face its troubled past and accept the continuity of German history. On October 3, 1990, eleven months after the fall of the wall, the country reunified with Berlin as its capital.

Now considered the outpost of the industrialized west in the emerging markets of the east, the city experienced an immediate boom. Huge investments were made in providing office space for the multinational companies expected to move their European headquarters to Berlin. Equally, the government began planning the new capital, disregarding completely the buildings the communist rulers had built as their own government seat. Unlike any other city experiencing a spurt in growth, much of

Berlin's geographical center—an empty band up to 500 feet wide—had been kept free of development. The "death strip" of the wall, once the most feared land in Europe, had become its most sought-after real estate.

In the city of Berlin, no two generations had lived under the same political system for nearly two centuries, and its people were as suspicious of the status quo as they were wary of change. For most aspects of life, including architecture, this meant avoiding references to past values that, for so much of Germany's history, had negative implications. To many it seemed more appropriate to work with strategies considered untainted than to sort through the troubled past in search of valuable remnants.

As an American firm, Moore Ruble Yudell had none of the hang-ups of its European colleagues. Part of the firm's credo is to work from the indigenous values of a site, to draw inspiration from what is special and beautiful in a given context. Based in California, where most stylistic expressions are imports, the architects were able in Berlin to refer to the past in a natural way: neither as pretense, nor as commentary. When MRY won the

11

commission for the lakefront Berliner Strasse housing,[11] the typology of neighboring 18th century villas by Schinkel and Persius inspired a certain scale and language: design strategies of adding simple volumes to create complex shapes and juxtaposing solid masses with lighter elements.

Despite this strategy of assimilation, the design faced some obstacles. A number of similarly scaled projects had met the opposition of preservationists who feared that the area, a historic landscape design, would encounter too much development. UNESCO even threatened to revoke Potsdam's status as a world heritage site if this and other projects were built; fortunately, the challenge was later reworded to exclude Berliner Strasse.

Like every architectural project in Berlin, the design for Berliner Strasse was also closely scrutinized by the public. With a general population very interested in all aspects of the physical environment, Berlin's media cater to design to such an extent that architecture makes the front pages of the newspapers on a regular basis. It gradually became evident in the reports that Moore Ruble Yudell, while

always referred to as "the California firm of …," enjoyed a status somewhat different from that of the other international competitors. Tegel Harbor had made its mark on pre-unification Berlin, and MRY was regarded by some as a local firm. This was helped by the frequent presence in the city of principals John Ruble and Buzz Yudell, who, in their quest to untangle the place they had grown to love, had engaged in weekly German lessons when at home in California.

While private development was well on its way to exceeding demand, the German government had yet to fulfill one of its biggest unification promises. East Germany had been suffering from a blatant need for housing. It was even said that couples whose marriages had failed would not file for divorce in fear of losing their housing privileges. The Federal and State governments embarked on a multi-billion dollar housing campaign that invoked the settlement building of the 1920s. Private developers were equipped with subsidies and engaged in public–private partnerships to develop a multitude of housing projects, including a number of new towns within the periphery.

Under this system, the state covers much of the construction cost, while the developer implements the project. As owner, the developer is subject to strict building standards and is required to rent the units to eligible low- and moderate-income tenants at controlled rates. After thirty years (the same period as for much publicly subsidized housing in the United States), rent control expires and the units—built to last according to the regulations—become market rate housing.

Notwithstanding their general poverty, East Germans had enjoyed a number of constitutional rights that came with the communist ideology—among them the right to a job and to daycare for their children, so they could pursue their work without conflict. These rights, a mere dream for us in the West, expired with unification. In response to the resulting social tensions, local authorities often included community infrastructure such as schools and daycare centers in publicly funded projects.

MRY was invited to participate in design workshops for two of these publicly funded new communities: Kirchsteigfeld, near Potsdam, and Karow Nord, just outside Berlin. The Kirchsteigfeld master plan was largely designed by Rob Krier—with MRY as co-author—and MRY designed a number of individual new buildings. The learning process was painful at times. While Tegel had been subsidized housing, it was also eased along in development as an international showpiece, and Berliner Strasse was privately funded luxury housing. As tightly scrutinized public projects, Kirchsteigfeld and Karow presented a new challenge for the firm.

Germany's high standards for housing construction—load-bearing brick walls, poured-in-place slabs and staircases, wood windows with low-e glazing—require a high initial investment. Yet the typical developer's goal is to shave a profit off the subsidization funds, which are calculated strictly at cost. In this environment, any design element had to be inherent to the structure of the building, or it would be eliminated in the process.

Only months after being asked to participate in Kirchsteigfeld, MRY was also commissioned to design the master plan of Karow Nord and was subsequently placed at the center of political negotiations surrounding the largest

12

13

housing project in Berlin's history.[12] The task was daunting: implementing such a project would be quite an undertaking anywhere, but here the situation was enormously complicated by recent history.

In the project for Karow Nord, East truly met west on all levels. Karow lay within the outskirts of the formerly East German part of the city, like many new projects at the time. While the developers and government officials were from the west, the planning authorities were all East German. Within the team, the sense of cooperation was accompanied by suspicion and misunderstanding as well. When MRY presented design guidelines to the other architects, the discussions often seemed off the mark.

At the time, no one tried to create the illusion that Germany was one country: there were still "Ossis" and "Wessis," and both groups spent much time complaining about how their lives had changed. Having grown up to mistrust one another, people from East and West Germany were now brought together by developers and politicians to implement a highly complex project—all under the direction of a foreign firm. While the West Berlin participants had grown used to a lack of authority, their eastern colleagues had been subjected to too many rules in the past and were unaccustomed to pluralist dispute. In an ironic show of unity, at times the reaction on both of their parts was stubborn refusal to adhere to any rules.

While Karow Nord was being constructed piece by piece,[13] Moore Ruble Yudell decided to pursue a very different project, and their first in Berlin for an American client. With the German government's move slowly taking shape, foreign nations started to reclaim their long-abandoned embassy properties. Before the war, the United States Embassy had enjoyed a prime spot between Pariser Platz, one of Berlin's primary squares, and the Tiergarten, its central park. Directly south of the Brandenburg Gate, its damaged building had been obliterated by the Soviet forces, but the vacant site remained United States property. The U.S. State Department was fully aware of the political importance of establishing a strong presence in the newly emerging Berlin when they embarked on the competition.

14

Besides fulfilling the myriad of technical and program requirements, the project's central challenge was to complement the urban context, including the Brandenburg Gate, while clearly establishing a presence in Berlin for the United States. The only competitor with a long-running engagement in the city, Moore Ruble Yudell produced a proposal that responded foremost to the context, both in design and social attitude. Its typology, a courtyard building, grew directly from German regulations requiring a window with an unobstructed view in every workplace. Seeking to enter into dignified dialogue with the surrounding landmarks, the building thus bears certain similarities to the architecture of the U.S. capital city. The potentially conflicting goals of complementing the context while symbolizing a foreign power is resolved with synergy. In the spring of 1996, the jury awarded the design first prize. For Moore Ruble Yudell, it felt like coming home to two places.

Late in the 20th century, Berlin seems finally to have achieved the goals of "unity, justice, and freedom" expressed in the first line of the 1841 German national anthem.[14] At the beginning of the new millennium, the new capital stands the chance of emerging as a true world city if it overcomes its trauma and preserves its openness; if it sorts through its past—good and bad—and uses this knowledge to create a place undivided.

PROJECT

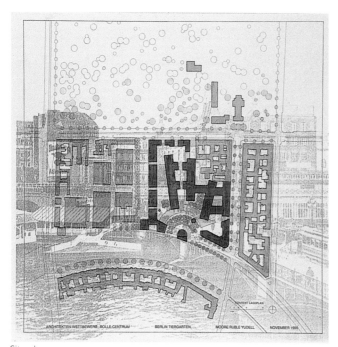

Site plan

A proposal for a mixed-use development in Berlin, near the Tiergarten and facing the Spree Canal, called for approximately 90,000 square meters of primarily new office space adjacent to a historical warehouse building, the Meierei.

The site is entered by passing through large arcades in existing buildings along the Alt Moabit, a busy collector street. The scheme proposes four long, narrow buildings of seven, nine and eleven stories loosely paralleling the Meierei, splayed slightly to suggest a center point across the Spree. Each building steps down with outdoor terraces to a winter garden greenhouse that curves in plan, and contains cafes, shops, and gardens.

View from river

BOLLE CENTER

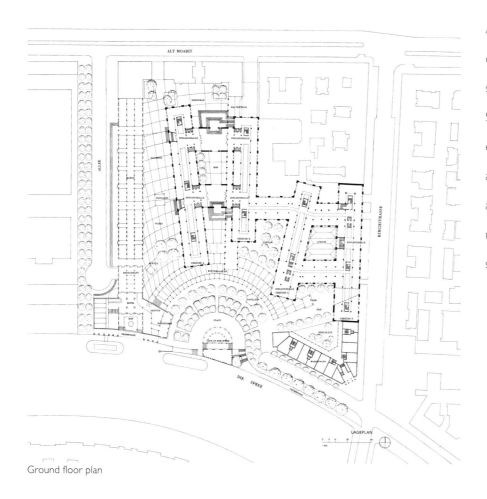

Ground floor plan

A major public plaza is shaped by a glassy colonnade and rows of trees; at its heart is a small restored industrial building against the Spree. The former Meierei office is now expanded with canopies into a festival hall and cafe, and the whole complex sits on one-and-a-half stories of underground parking. A new 100-unit housing block anchors the southeast corner along the Spree.

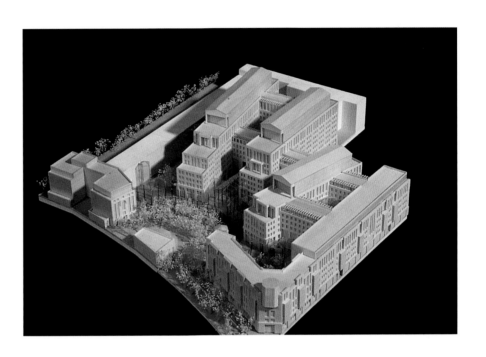

View along riverfront

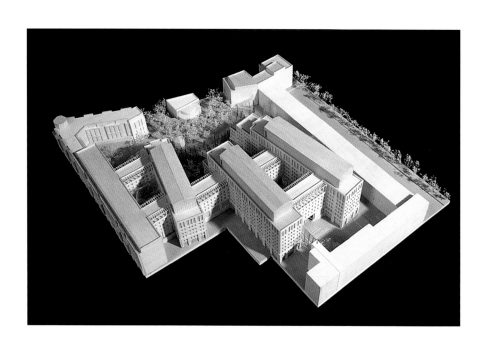

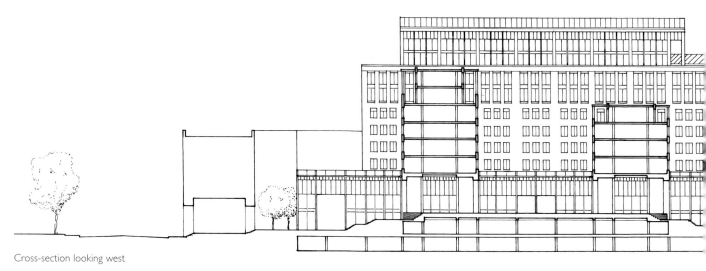

Cross-section looking west

BOLLE CENTER

The proposal recalls the strong unadorned vernacular of 19th century industrial buildings and market halls: walls sheathed with brick and the generous use of steel and glass for atria, lobbies, and gathering places. The long, stepped profiles of the four buildings and the Meierei make an elegant skyline of temple-like glass facades and terraces from the Spree. The spaces between the buildings support a variety of active commercial and quiet garden uses. The central plaza presents a major event along the river: an urbane public park connected to the existing waterside pedestrian ways.

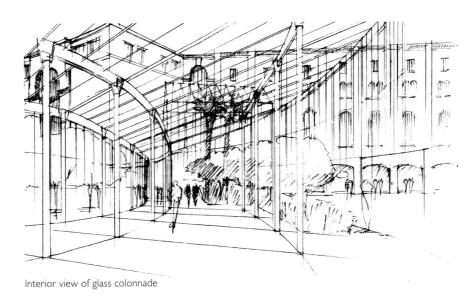

Interior view of glass colonnade

PROJECT

FRIEDRICHSTADT PASSAGEN

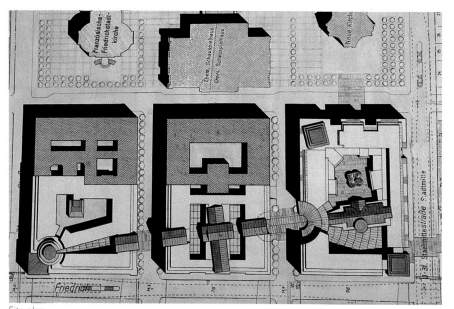
Site plan

The challenge of MRY's proposal for a three-block stretch at the heart of East Berlin was to set the tone for new urban development in the unified Germany. The site, located in the Mitte district of Berlin and adjacent to the historic Schauspielhaus and Akademie-platz, has been the focus of significant debate since reunification.

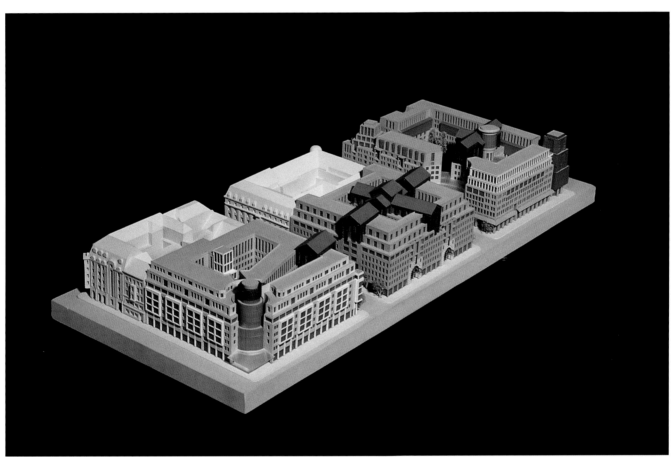

Model view along Friedrichstrasse

View looking northeast

The project includes a 225-room hotel overlooking Akademieplatz; 90 housing units on the upper levels; 28,000 square meters of specialty retail space; a department store; 63,000 square meters of office space; a 14-theater cinema complex with food court; and, at the rooftop level, looking out across the city, a city building museum for the display and discussion of future projects for Berlin.

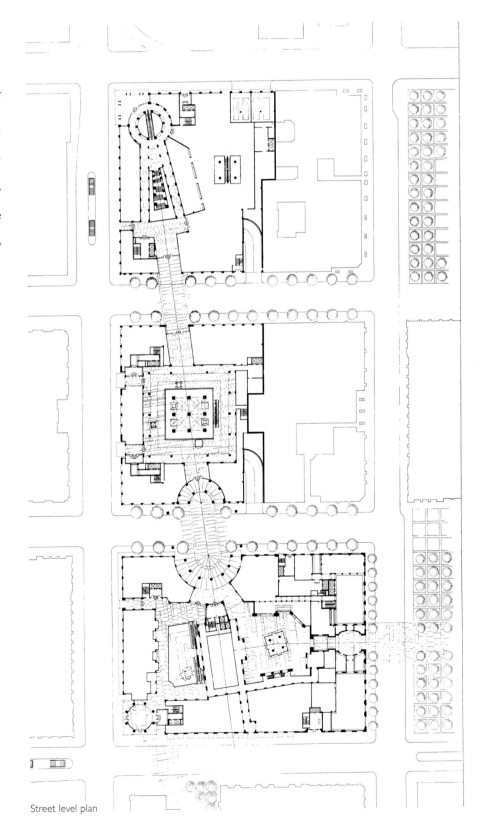

Street level plan

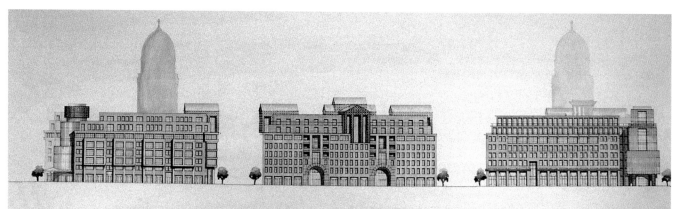

Elevation model along Friedrichstrasse

Section model showing atria and lower floor connection

All three blocks are linked by a single pedestrian passage at street and concourse levels. This passage establishes a series of important public spaces within the project, without sacrificing maximum density for the surrounding uses. At the core of each block, a principal room along the passage connects all levels vertically, rising from the stone floor of the lower level. Each one has a thematic focus that is particular to the block. These pieces create an aura of theater around the busy movement of people, transforming the traditional passage of pre-war Berlin into a contemporary forum for urban life.

Interior view of south atrium

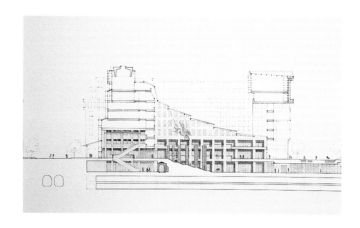

Atria sections

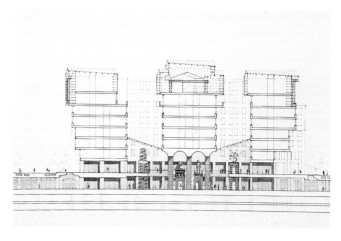

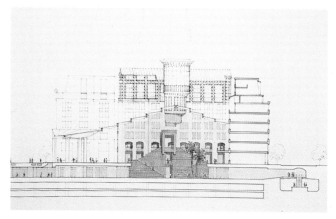

View of rooftop exhibition space

PROJECT

PEEK & CLOPPENBURG

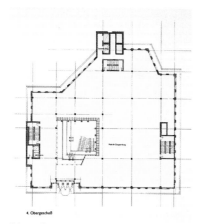

Upper floor

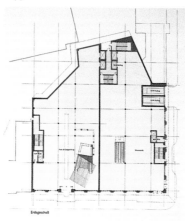

Ground floor

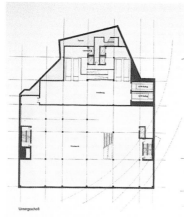

Basement

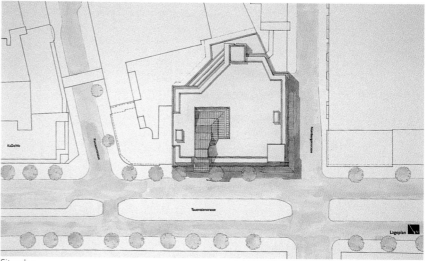

Site plan

The German department store chain Peek & Cloppenburg sought to replace its existing Berlin flagship department store on Tauentzien Strasse, very near the famous "Ka De We." The building includes 27,000 square meters on seven floors: five for retail merchandising and two for offices.

Due to leasing arrangements with Woolworths, with whom the site was to be jointly developed, the site issues were complex. Consequently, the building is designed to allow its own eventual division into separate establishments.

Opposite: Interior view of glass atrium

PEEK & CLOPPENBURG

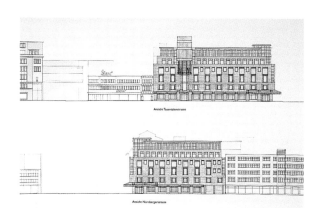

Main entrance and side elevations

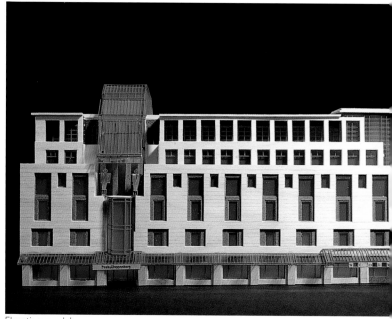

Elevation model

Shoppers, drawn through the ground floor by natural light and glimpses of a skylit atrium above, ascend the escalators or grand stair to mezzanine level. The retail floors are focused on the large second-level central space. Careful choices of materials, details, and color subtly enhance the display of merchandise through the dramatic consideration of artificial and natural light and space.

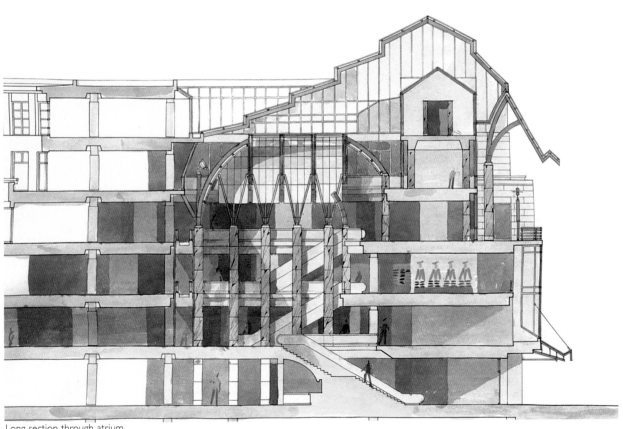

Long section through atrium

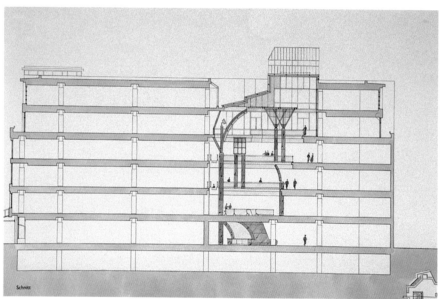

Atrium cross-section

View of ground floor entry sequence

BERLINER STRASSE HOUSING

Existing Kampfmeyer Villa

The site for 75 luxury condominiums is situated southwest of Berlin at the gateway to Potsdam, lying at the center of a network of pastoral views between 19th century Neoclassical palaces and Baroque downtown Potsdam. Twelve individual villas are designed to complement and frame a rather large existing restored villa, and relate to the delicate and more refined scale of historic buildings by Schinkel and his colleague Persius, visible nearby. The buildings contain three to ten units each, and share contiguous underground parking.

Site plan with Glienicker Bridge

BERLINER STRASSE HOUSING

The site plan is divided into three distinct areas: a cluster of villas at the entry arranged around open lawns; a formal landscaped court adjacent to the existing villa, defined by arcades and symmetrical facades; and a new canal-like marina leading to the Havel, with houses tight against it to frame a dramatic view of water and parkland beyond.

The new villas, while comparable in scale to the existing 19th century house, use pergolas, pavilions, and roof gardens to establish a range of scales and connections with the landscape. Their massing combines rational volumes and picturesque compositions, recalling especially memorable aspects of the "Potsdam Style." Traditional materials—stone bases, stucco walls, and tile roofs—are embellished with layers of glassy towers, bays, and loggias to bring the fleeting hours of sunlight deep into the units.

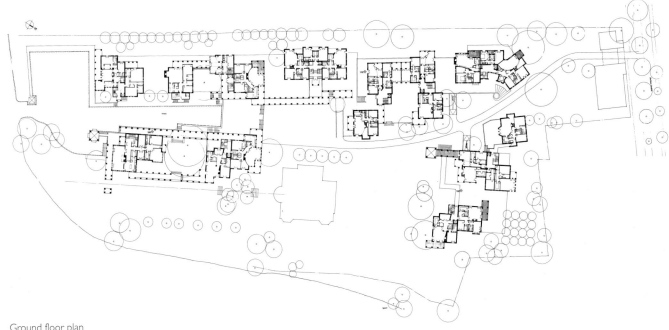

Ground floor plan

villas and pergolas defining courtyard

The units are a mix of small, medium, and large types that balance the formality of Neoclassical plans with the informality of 20th century open plan interiors. A language of great rooms with bays and inglenooks creates a variety of special unit plans while maintaining the continuity of the elevations.

The landscape design is derived similarly from the idea of a set of pieces—pergolas, penthouses, and garden rooms—that connect the freestanding villas and recall their illustrious neighbors.

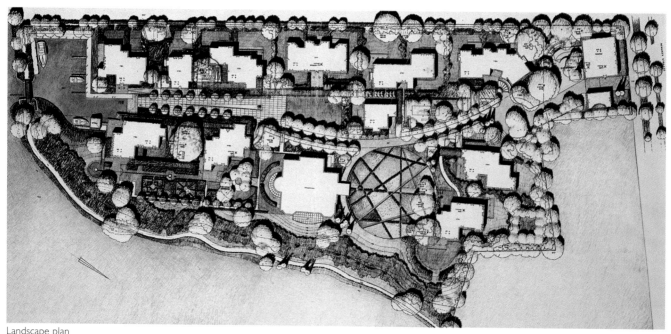

Landscape plan

BERLINER STRASSE HOUSING

Following pages: Garden path along
western edge of site

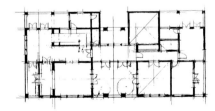

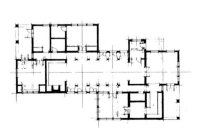

Development of plan and massing:
the addition of elements

Gatehouse from the site

Opposite: Gatehouse from the street

BERLINER STRASSE HOUSING

Scales of Habitation

by Buzz Yudell

Shaping new communities *de novo* is one of the most thrilling and daunting challenges for an architect and urbanist. Unlike designing a single house for an individual client, the architect is familiar with the future inhabitants only through a range of approximations and intuitions. The most vital communities we know and study have usually developed over many generations, and embody a vernacular and evolutionary wisdom in their urban fabric. Composing high-density multiple-unit housing patterns offers the opportunity to create, over time, authentic dwelling places for individuals, families, groups, and communities.

The anti-community would be a monoculture in its physical, social, and environmental characteristics. A successful new community would be rich in its variety of occupants, places, architectural typologies, scales, and social opportunities. It would allow for a strong sense of its own identity, while establishing sympathetic connections to its surrounding context and environment. It would embody diversity and choice, surprise and delight, and yet possess coherent underlying principles of organization and growth: a kind of urban genetic code that would allow for orderly and diverse growth but also avert chaotic metastasis.

For these and other reasons, it is not surprising that most utopian, idealized or master-planned communities have suffered various degrees of failure. Typically, the deficiencies arise out of a lack of complexity and diversity. On the "high art" side of the spectrum (Brasilia and Chandigarh, for example), the fault is due to an overly diagrammatic urban conception that, in spite of the varied success of individual powerful buildings, averts any organic success for the place as a city or community. In the realm of much current private sector development, the loss of value usually stems from a foundation of "exclusivist" planning, often based on preoccupations with security and marketing. Gated communities, generated from desires for security, safety and avoidance of the "messy" complexity of urbanism, represent segregated enclaves suffocating from a lack of cultural and economic diversity, connection, and interchange.

Diversity and Choice

We feel that there can be alternatives to the extremes of abstract utopian or prosaic monocultural enclaves. The vitality of our civic life, indeed the vibrancy of a democratic society, is integrally related to our culture's ability to create and sustain diverse and humane communities. Essential to establishing richly inhabited new communities is the creation of diversity and choice, in as many dimensions as possible. The community should be diverse in economic, social, and cultural patterns. While the architect and planner have only partial ability to control these variables, choice should be fostered both physically and programmatically. Architecture and urbanism can go far toward developing neighborhoods and towns that present a rich array of types of places to inhabit, and which are shaped to stimulate and support human interaction. The vitality of our civic life, indeed the vibrancy of a democratic society, is integrally related to our culture's ability to create and sustain diverse and humane communities.

Scales of Habitation

One of the most powerful tools we have found in our search to create such places is the idea of scales of habitation. This concept is central to our conception and design of new communities. At its core it is a commitment to the notion that we need to dwell in and understand our place in the world at multiple scales simultaneously. One can describe many different spatial hierarchies: global, regional, local; or country, city, town, district, neighborhood, block, street, building, apartment. The precise terminology is perhaps not so important as the idea that each scale presents a physical, perceptual, and psychological realm of inhabitation. In architectural terms, each scale should be conceived so that we may understand and experience our individual and shared presence in that construct. Further, each scale is linked to every other scale in a dynamic nexus of relationships.

Reading the Present and the Past

Studying the site and sensing the place constitute the first step in our urban planning process. This involves reading a wide array of complex landscape and settlement patterns, both physical and typological. In the new town of Karow Nord, we found the allegedly "greenfield" site was, in fact, inscribed with a complex set of tracings of activity. Roughly bow-tie-shaped, the site existed in relation to a diverse set of adjacent pressures and connections. It is bisected by a north–south road that becomes the main identity and artery of the old town of Karow to the south. To the north is the elevated autobahn and high-density block housing. To the east is primarily agricultural land; to the south, the historic and delicately scaled village of Karow; to the west, a regional rail link and additional housing.

1

2

3

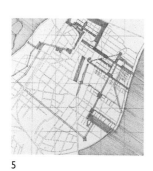

4

5

Weaving into the Region

While Karow Nord is a new town of 5,000 housing units, its planning is woven into the highly diverse fabric of its neighbors.[1] The existing network of paths and significant landscape features was the starting point for the town's geometric armature. The highly inflected and differentiated street network is itself a complex synthesis, linking to existing neighbors at multiple scales, and accommodating different modes and speeds of movement. Its underlying geometry is an orthogonal block pattern related to neighboring typologies, which is varied locally to create careful linkages with adjacent areas.[2] Key diagonal paths further connect major internal foci and allow for "short-cut" paths to existing neighborhoods.[3] More than ten different street types are derived in close conformity to the social, spatial, and circulation needs of their districts, and allow for further differentiation and identity.[4]

In a similar fashion, we worked with Knippschild Müller to develop an equally complex pattern of landscaped open spaces that connect with and speak to existing adjacencies, and also create identifiable figures for the new project. Some of these figures are focal spaces that help to establish a distinct identity for different neighborhoods. Others are linear connectors, such as the east–west greens that link to the historic agrarian patterns of the fields to the east.[5] Certain irregularly shaped spaces such as the Auepark in the west occur "opportunistically" where shifted grids meet.[6] The elongated lozenge shape of the "Querspange" serves as both an identifiable focal space for the whole community and as a linking element to help overcome the bifurcated geometry of the site as a whole.

Housing and Block Typologies

The hierarchy of streets and open spaces is coordinated with a hierarchy of block and housing typologies that create spatial, social, and environmental diversity. City blocks are dimensioned to allow a set of private, semi-private, semi-public, and public zones. Carefully studied in plan and section, and in relationship to solar orientation and the nature of adjacent uses, more than twenty block types and five major housing types are woven into a highly articulated fabric. Perimeter blocks allow for higher densities and protected inner courtyards. Mixed-use terraces border important linking spaces such as the Querspange. "Villas" containing multiple apartment units constitute highly individuated

6

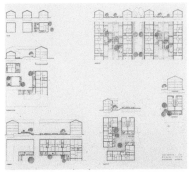

7

8

9

10

housing along important diagonal boulevards or fronting on special landscape and water elements. "Karow Courts," modeled on the spatial relationships of houses in the old village, provide multi-unit housing at a transitional scale that seeks to "feather" the new community into its neighboring village. Finally, agrarian row houses make scale-sensitive linkages to the south and east.

Scales of Community and Privacy

Within each block, the sectional relationship through each housing type and its associated open spaces is highly articulated, and bears directly on the quality of habitation of every unit, house, courtyard, and neighborhood.[7] The resulting grain and hierarchy are quite tangible: streets that are lively, porches that are open but protected, yards and gardens that occupy the transition between community and privacy, and even parking that animates streets and courts. Given that most of the housing in Karow Nord is social housing with modestly scaled apartments of 45 to 95 square meters, these transitional zones of habitation are exceptionally important in humanizing the place of living, and giving a sense of individual and shared identity.[8]

Community Uses and Amenities

Critical to the vitality of any community is a rich mix of opportunities and uses. It was essential to our success as architects and urbanists that we were working within a culture that understands and supports the importance of a diverse mixed-use community designed to integrate itself into the greater context. At Karow Nord we were able to site schools and "kitas" strategically,[9] at neighborhood nodes within walking distance of the students' and parents' homes. By including commercial, office, and civic uses within the residential matrix, the Querspange becomes not only a physical link between the eastern and western neighborhoods, but a focus of community life. Intersected, in turn, by the old north–south Karow road, the new center also relates to old Karow's core, and beyond to adjacent towns. Here, we were able to structure a physical nexus that is given life by the programmatic diversity that the government and developers were willing to support. The civic uses, of course, were subsidized and even the "commercial" uses were understood as necessary community-building elements that might not be immediately profitable.[10]

A Culture of Community

During the design phase of Karow Nord, we were asked to participate in a colloquium with several other architects, each presenting their urban design for a current project in greater Berlin. Rushing through the Tiergarten on the evening of the event with our Berlin associate, Miller Stevens, I wondered aloud if there would be more than a handful of planners in the audience, since we were all presenting urban planning and there would not be the usual seductive images of buildings upon which architects typically fixate. To my amazement, we entered the hall to find the space packed with a lively array of people engaged in animated conversation, sipping drinks and studying a display of planning documents for the projects. While mostly dressed in stylish black turtlenecks, jeans and jackets, they were a diverse group: from young students to professionals of all ages. At home, only presentations by the most avant-garde form-makers would draw such a group.

As always in Berlin, discussion during the following colloquium was intense and at times highly polarized, but it revealed that these were people who cared passionately about the city—past, present and future. This diverse group clearly represented a city and culture deeply committed to the process of planning for and shaping community.

German Lessons

While we hope that we, as American and Californian architects, have brought some fresh dimensions to shaping communities in Berlin, we are certain that Berlin brings lessons for us. We found three of those lessons from Berlin especially important.

First, I would posit that architects must not abdicate the civic conversation. Too often we retreat to the relative protection of working with the few private clients who recognize the artistic importance of our work. While the more public arena is a daunting tangle of argument and bureaucracy, our collective professional participation is essential.

Next, we can take inspiration from a culture that still understands the value of weaving civic life into our neighborhoods. The street and the plaza, the market and the school are essential to a humane and democratized urban life.

Last, we should note that major civic commitments must be structured by some form of public–private partnership. In Karow Nord the planning process began with a civic commitment to create 5,000 housing units to help address the needs of the newly reunited East. It proceeded based on incentives to private developers. But throughout, there was a creative, if sometimes contentious and always delicate, balance of public and private interests.

The shaping of community is an arduous task involving the participation of innumerable stakeholders. Its complexity is at times overwhelming. The inevitable competing interests can threaten and diminish the initial visions. However, the team of architects, landscape architects, planners, and other designers can play a vital role in shaping places that enhance human habitation. When considered at multiple scales and dimensions, this process offers us the opportunity to develop richly wrought neighborhoods that support civic life and help to build vital and diverse communities.

KIRCHSTEIGFELD

As a result of the intense growth initiated since the reunification of Germany, a field located near historic Potsdam was to be developed into a new town providing the full complement of civic, commercial, and residential uses, including 2,500–3,000 housing units, 160,000 square meters of commercial uses, two elementary schools, one high school, a sports center, and public parks and services.

Competition entry by MRY: site plan

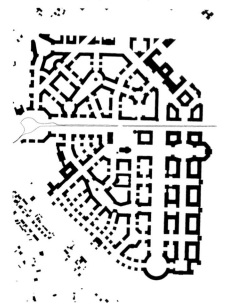

Final design of winning entry by Krier and Kohl with MRY

Streetscape

The site represents a microcosm of the issues facing development in East Germany since reunification. On one side sits a small 700-year-old village overrun by burgeoning traffic headed into Berlin; on the other side, Neue Siedlungen provides an all-too-common reminder of the brutalism of postwar planning. The third side is carved by the autobahn, representing both a positive link to the larger Germany and the negative impact of noise and pollution. Between them all is Kirchsteigfeld.

Intersection marked by tower buildings

Composite street elevation by participating architects

In addition to working with Rob Krier and Christoph Kohl in refining the master plan for the 53-hectare site, MRY was asked to design 250 units in 20 buildings distributed across the new town. Moore Ruble Yudell's contribution to the Krier urban scheme—which emphasized a formal, enclosed block structure, a strong figure/ground contrast, and tight urban spaces—was largely to loosen up the rather strict diagram, and to open view portals and pedestrian passages into the housing blocks.

Mid-block housing type

Villa housing type

Following pages: Corner housing

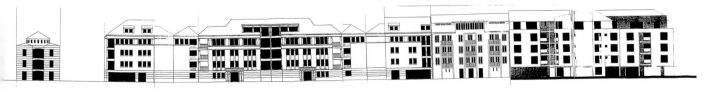

Mid-block housing

Opposite: Corner housing at linear park

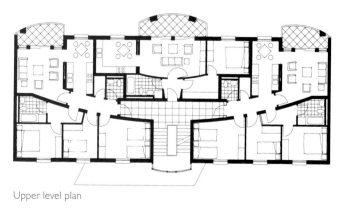

Upper level plan

Housing facing pond

The MRY housing includes several corner sites, mid-block sites, and a villa, as well as the curved centerpiece buildings of the first major green space. Building footprints were stipulated, for the most part, as were roof pitches and eave heights.

Following pages: Corner housing

Interior courtyard

Linear park

With buildings by many different architects possessing sometimes very different styles, the MRY approach called for quiet restraint and a deference to the larger order of streets and squares. In their various locations, the buildings possess some similarities and common themes, but are largely allowed to relate to their particular site and immediate context in both massing and details. A consistent architectural *parti* of base, middle, and top, with occasional horizontal striping and pilasters, provides a common sense of scale and articulation. Depending on their site conditions, however, some buildings are more "object-like" and others more "background" in character. The location of major elements such as corner bays and balconies responds both to the streetscape and to views from afar, across the park.

The understated vocabulary of facade elements is enhanced by a color palette derived from historical examples in nearby Potsdam.

Mid-block building: street elevation

Courtyard side

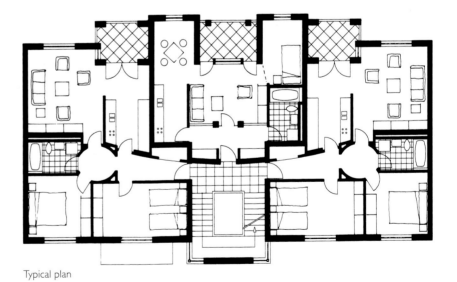

Typical plan

The Warp and the Woof

By Dan Garness

Memo: May 24, 1994

To: Miller Stevens

From: Dan Garness

Dear Miller

Please call immediately.

—Dan

The Berlin projects are by and large conducted by fax. In between bi-monthly visits, faxes structure the process, every day or other, with phone calls to follow-up on faxed information. We send birthday, wedding, and christening greetings by fax to keep the relationships visual and tactile, as well as touch-tone aural. Some of these greetings are perhaps still pinned to a wall in the Brunnenstrasse or in Kreuzberg. The whole MRY team signs them, just to cast our net as widely as possible.

Faxes from Berlin can be pored over in meetings, marked up with impunity, wadded in frustration (copies to everyone), filed exultantly. Drawings from MRY are faxed in long strips to short-cut the Fedex window. The Berliner Strasse schematics are faxed in one curfew-busting marathon machine-feeding the first night of the 1992 Los Angeles riots. By fax we discuss the 1994 earthquake with Miller, and Robert Altman's *Short Cuts*, with its timely facsimile earthquake wrapping up several L.A. storylines. *Deux ex machina*, indeed.

Memo: August 31, 1994

To Miller Stevens

From: Dan Garness

Dear Miller

This weekend will be a long weekend (Friday off and Monday is Labor Day—they're all long and every day is labor day, no?). So can we make one more stab at uncovering the Karow cornerstone story? Let's talk when you are able so we can finally get these ducks in a row, as shown:

⟨duck symbols⟩ . . .

Berliner Strasse

Materials at hand:

- Schinkel & Persius villas and castles nearby, firm massing, delicate scale.

- Streetscape across the Karower Chaussée consisting of moderate 19th century villas with elegantly proportioned balconies, sunrooms, roof terraces.

- The River Havel, historic arbiter of view corridors and environmental connections between Potsdam monuments—Neoclassical skyline, picturesque settings. Sweet waterway into channels and lakes, grounding the landscape in a floating world of perfectly proportioned facades and deep green clouds of trees.

- 1990s program of large expensive units, as many as will fit.

The design begins with three massing concepts presented to the client and Herr Rohrbein, Potsdam head planner, who encourage a street-like configuration of individual villas and a possible water event— a canal or quay—off the Havel. We outline a set of architectural and landscape image-elements borrowed from the neighborhood—pergolas, porches, green allées, raised lawn terraces—which may be combined, referred to. One Sunday the scheme coalesces, stacked and pinned foamcore, into a row of similarly sized buildings with bay windows and rooftop gazebos: a picturesque overlay to the repetitive massing. A repertory of architectural shapes develops, and an enthusiastic exploitation of the site: two mirrored towers mark a gateway to an axial harbor; a single small villa ends the view from the water; a cluster of houses adhere to a common lawn. The entry from Berliner Strasse passes under a low-arched gatehouse, which gives a view to the designated touchstone in the midst of the property— the existing, historic Kampfmeyer Villa. The question: how to provide an order to the proceedings?

Looking back to Charles' Sea Ranch, and the shadow of Kahn behind it, we develop a system of square plans with bays or saddle-bags, 12 meters on a side, with 1.5-meter by 3 meter articulations. The latter make porches, *wintergartens*, entries, stair halls, and elevator cores. The additions specify the massing and skyline, masking and revealing the underlying rhythm of general shapes. Unit plans are fused with the overall site plan; repeated curved-wall living spaces unify views into and across the site and provide a rhythmic counterpoint of indoor and outdoor public spaces. Shared gardens and rooftop terraces populate the landscape. All the scheme needs is some sensitive detailing, kindness from strangers such as the building department, and we are there.

There is the territory of a design which falls naturally, progressively into place, and also (importantly) survives the daily rigors of passing through the hands of others not present at its inception. The program threads are identified, sorted, arranged into patterns, layed over and particularized by the site, and made into something whole and of a piece, which then must be expanded and tested by other teams, other experts. We hope for like-minded collaborators and happy accidents. There is a time for the coming together of ideas, and, like football, a time for defense.

To: Miller Stevens

From: Dan Garness

Dear Miller

In advance of attending the Berliner Strasse meeting Thursday (thankyouthankyouthankyouthankyou), I'd like to give you a short synopsis of the plot to date, as follows:

Nov 1991 Project starts, PSP as associated architects.

Jun 1992 Design development complete, PSP to begin work.

(Note: We provided several different unit plans, both larger and smaller, at each villa, based on Dieter Graalfs' comments before finalizing design.)

1993 Zoning plan approved based on MRY site plan.

Building permit drawings done by PSP, keeping strictly to our massing, and using many of our unit plans.

Jan 1994 Bodin hired to replace PSP, revises some unit plans and massing, making larger units (similar in size to our original unit plans). No attempt made to contact MRY.

May 1994 John and Miller Stevens meet with Bodin et. al. at G+G. Plans to be sent to MRY.

Jun/July 1994 Plans arrive very slowly, incomplete in some areas—no site plan coordinating various plan changes.

July 1994 MRY send mark-up set of Bodin's drawings indicating and commenting on all conditions (massing, elevation, and plans) which have been changed.

July/Aug 1994 MRY sends revision sketches for Villas E & G, C & H. Note: Villa A still requires significant revisions; no drawings yet received for office building or for elevations of several villas; no site plan.

Aug 1994 G+G dealing with problems of water table at site, poor market response. Propose no garage (surface parking). This is rejected by City.

Aug/Sept 1994 Back to square $1\frac{1}{2}$.

Your honor, I rest my case.

Working by fax is both time-consuming and truncated. Sometimes, like a disappointing restaurant (food is bad and portions too small), the answers come late and there just aren't enough of them.

The design has a lifespan. It bursts forward in excitement at the scale of the site, the honorable location, the chance to do innovative interiors. It must then survive, interact with multiple viewpoints (even at one point Prince Charles'!), a pluralist society of planners, critics, and buyers. There is a secret language of geometry and posture to hold the site, a dignified resilience. As Stravinsky suggests in his *Poetics of Music*, we use a tightly restricted set of design elements combined with invention to achieve harmony and diversity with a minimum of means. We hope for aesthetic transparency and good sales.

We open the process to the opinions of inspired planners such as Herr Rohrbein and Dieter Graalfs with the hope that the system is strong enough to inherit their images of the site too. Charles suggested that bread cast upon the water returned as club sandwiches. (Stravinsky asked for camembert.) We get in this case butter and brie on a bun—extravagantly caloric, and does it work?

Memo: January 5, 1994

To: Miller Stevens
From: Dan Garness
Dear Miller
It is essential that I speak to you. I've been trying to reach you by phone for three days. I must have your assistance in reviewing the B-Plan Test. Trouble is brewing.
Please call.
Yours
Karow Nord
Materials at hand:

- The legacy of *Siedlungen* planning and design, including: early 20th century romantic suburbs; Bruno Taut's color-wealthy developments of the 20s; the still-fresh discoveries of the 1970s IBA program; and the astoundingly failed example of East German 10-story slab towers (one group of which is distressingly close-by).

- The district scale of the Berlin ring-road autobahn—which oddly enough is not the projected main route to the city center; this remains the older crooking two-lane Karower Chaussée, a traffic engineer's advertisement for emergency by-pass surgery.

- The sylvan, still-preserved, open agricultural fields surrounding.

- Karow the village, with a lovely central *kern* or village green lined with historic villas (only slightly decayed) and farm outbuildings (converted to machine shops and convenience stores).

- The charming country-quilt of small cottages and attached *sommergarten* havens which dot the land.

Housing in Berlin is a fluid affair. Roommates move in and out at an alarming rate, apartments are held onto through deaths and divorces and restocked with new subtenants. No one seems ever to be living alone or accompanied for very long, and unlikely rooms are converted to habitable at the flick of a switch. Unit plans must and should be flexible, accommodating, surprising. One of the central tenets in the master planning of the Karow Nord project is that of choice: the ability to be upwardly or downwardly mobile within the same community, and also to choose the type of building-sized community or typology one wants to share.

The modest local housing examples suggest to us three typological models (in ascending order of scale): small individual cottages; "agrarian row houses" (two-story townhouses with attached gardens); and "Karow courts" (a cluster of one villa and two L-shaped buildings, with a shared courtyard and small private gardens). Two denser typologies come from central Berlin: large multi-unit villas, and four-story perimeter block apartment buildings. The range of typologies gives us the ability to sculpt the overall density of housing, as well as the texture of public–private space, segueing from tiny *sommergartens* to large mid-block lawns and playgrounds.

The traffic pattern is sculpted also. Every street and lane which abuts the site is brought into it, stitched in tight to allow every existing pathway to find its way to the new green interior. A hierarchy of major and minor roads further structure the housing density and provide focal points—*Plätze*—for gathering and urban emphasis. A striped pattern of long green spaces is laid over the street pattern to connect the new urban spaces to the existing countryside. We create and explain to associated Berlin architects the urban design, architectural, and color guidelines which support and enhance the scheme.

Memo: July 8, 1994
To: Miller Stevens
From: Dan Garness
Dear Miller

Just a few words about the upcoming Karow color meeting, and the hopefully resilient color concepts we are presenting. I show in italics some handy phrases which you might toss around.

Tina has done a wonderful job of restricting and *diverging* the palettes, and this comes across well in the presentation. The issue of *Hauptraumfolge* and how to show it graphically will need a little salesmanship. The concept as we discussed it today is I think sound, and moreover, correct. The idea of following a pathway which connects major spaces in a formal way, while allowing the experience of the connecting streets and walks to be rich and varied, according to the types of buildings and neighborhoods one is passing, is a direct extension of our original urban concepts. We have always stated the importance of *overlaying* and *balancing* large and small scales—a general grid-like fabric with formal pathways laid over it; diversity of architectural design and typology balanced with agreement in general character and in the streets and spaces created. The color concept furthers this "*regulating concept*" of the contrast of urban qualities—in this case, *"local pattern" of color, overlaid with larger scale color "events"*. Karow Nord is, I would think, too modest to suggest grand and overly diagrammatic color treatments of these simple *Plätze* and their subtle connections.

I am including a revised Color Guidelines Text (which Adrian had no time to translate). If you have the time it would be good to pass it out in German; otherwise perhaps you could have it on hand for a clear description of the *Farbengruppen* and how they relate to the architectural typologies.

Good luck in the meeting and aftermath. And, as Fred Astaire said to Ginger Rogers waiting in the wings, "Now don't be nervous, and don't make any mistakes." Or … break a leg.
Yours,

Urban design and site design are not about objects *per se*. They more resemble a kind of large-scale optical art with dots and dashes that the eye fuses together to make a complex whole. The items themselves exist on their own, but require the thoughtful gaze of the spectator and timely knowledge of the inhabitant to come together in the mind. The meaning of urbanity, if it can be gauged, is in the shifting relationships between coherent objects and open spaces—the intervals, not just the notes. These relationships are constructed in a time–space of familiar parameters, seen and reseen in unfamiliar ways. Each inhabitant carries the connections within, tacitly agreeing to acknowledge and make use of the implied civic whole.

The process is allusive. We use the timely memory of past devices to bring structure to the new and partly strange particulars of context. An old pattern is made into a new garment, loosely fitted, with perhaps clever and clairvoyant accessorizing. We use the aesthetic technique of *verbal collage*, multiple opinions being better than one, one generous size fitting many. As with any aging process, we hope for a little structural elasticity, a few hidden buttons in the waistline. We fight for the right to keep the ball rolling. In Berlin and elsewhere, this is how we have come to work.

I have learned two important new German words: *Gelassenheit* and *schlagfertig* ("serenity" and "quick at repartee"). In the bringing together of disparate pieces—uniting, patterning, and accommodating, and then guarding the strengths and subtleties of the design as it has a chance to coalesce—both are valuable. As the well-tempered master plan dissolves in time to streets and yards and drawn curtains, old mail and birthdays, reflection and event, both are useful.

Memo: August 10, 1994

To: Miller Stevens
From: Dan Garness
Dear Miller
I enclose original and translated text for the Senat publication. I also enclose this cover sheet which can be used to clean the fax machine. It's been quite a while since you cleaned it, I'm sure, so here it goes:
ccccccccclllllllllleeeeeeeeeeeaaaaaaaaaaaaaiiiiiii
nnnnnnnnngggggggggggnnnnnnnnnooooooooooo
wwwwwwwwww!!!!!!!!!!!!!!!
(It's a service we offer.)
Yours, always
Dan

KAROW NORD

MRY master plan

To Moore Ruble Yudell, the sudden addition of a new 5,000-unit residential sector to the historic village of Karow represented both an imposing challenge and an important opportunity. The scale of development and the speed of design and construction inherently threatened to overwhelm the distinct existing qualities of landscape and townscape; yet the chance to compose a new urbanity—and in doing so to represent the values and lessons of a particular moment in Berlin's urban history—was unique.

Previous pages: Town center: buildings
in foreground by MRY

Opposite: Mixed-use buildings by MRY

Two principal motives underlie the master plan for Karow Nord: to establish a town-like setting that draws forth the character of the agrarian site; and to emphasize qualities of habitation at every scale. As one of the new and necessarily large-scale developments of Berlin's perimeter, Karow is designed to maintain the high standards of German housing without sacrificing the particulars of place or the complexities of urban experience.

Karow village is both connected and protected. The existing street system is organically continued into the new project and integrated hierarchically with a set of new parks and public facilities. Simultaneously, the areas between the historic core and the new development are expected to evolve and adapt over time.

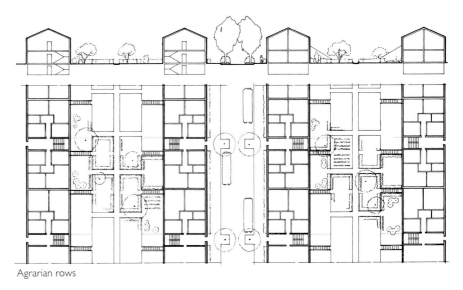

Agrarian rows

Following pages: Aue park

Above and below: Buildings in loose formation around the Aue park

Urban design guidelines are crucial for buildings and spaces to speak coherently, particularly when they are designed all at once. At Karow Nord, these guidelines are based on building types and are designed to encourage coherence within each residential district and contrast between districts. Color guidelines, based on typology, create large-scale harmonies and syncopations.

In the urban plan, schools, youth centers, and *kitas* are given significant positions and direct connections to green spaces. A series of linear parks and green boulevards draw the surrounding agrarian landscape deep into the new residential area. Housing is presented in five different building types—perimeter blocks, mixed-use terraces, villas, Karow Courts, and agrarian row houses—creating diversity and identity for both public places and private dwellings.

Buildings line the market garden

Karow Nord landscape: villa in foreground by MRY

A variety of street types, from small boulevard to country lane, are made as narrow as possible, allowing the automobile to function, but not dominate the street experience. A grand spatial sequence of axial streets and diagonals visually connects each of Karow Nord's main public places, providing a memorable order over the whole development.

Above and below: Varied scales and expressions

The Oval

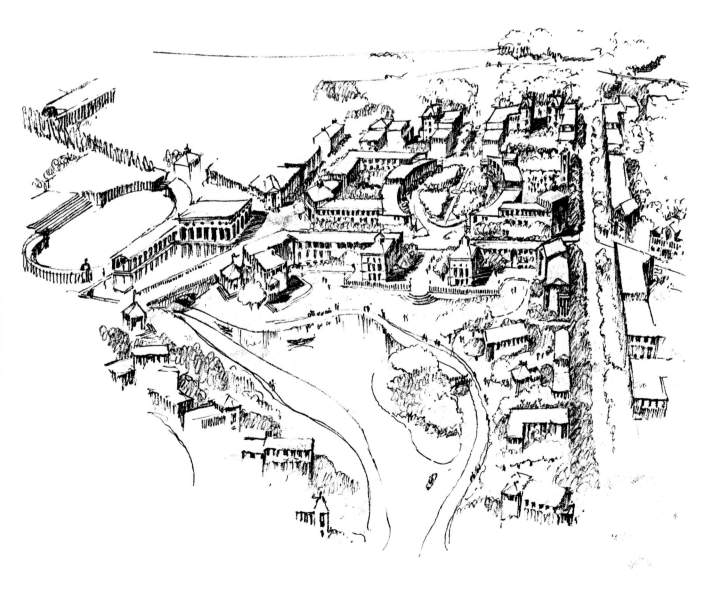

Perimeter blocks

Ground level plan

Following the adoption of the Karow Nord Master Plan, Moore Ruble Yudell was commissioned to complete several components of the town's extensive housing network—ranging from small-scale Karow Courts to large urban blocks—and several mixed-use buildings in the town center. These combine leasable retail space and offices with residential units on the upper floors.

Karow Court by MRY

Karow Court: building at left by MRY

Karow Courts

Ground level plan

Mid-block pedestrian path

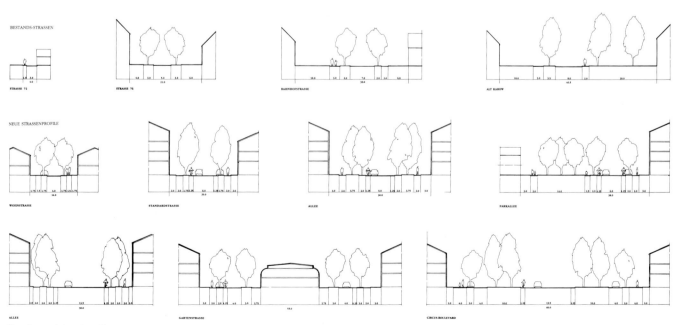

Typology of street sections

Public infrastructure: one of seven child daycare centers by various architects

Public infrastructure: high school library

Previous pages: Public infrastructure:
northern crescent of town center

Building by MRY occupied by Lutheran parish

Town center: retail

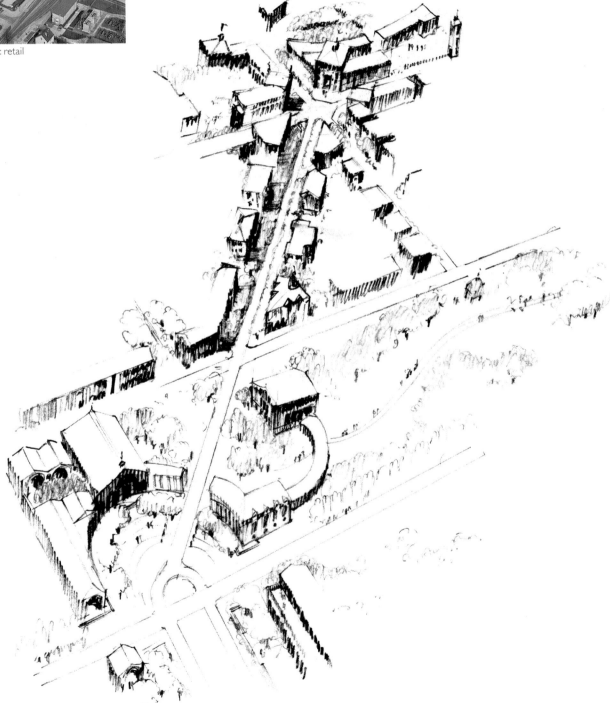

Opposite: Town center: retail below, office and housing above

PROJECT

TIERGARTEN DREIECK

Master plan by Machleidt + Stepp

The Tiergarten Dreieck is one of the last large contiguous building sites in the center of Berlin. Located just south of the Tiergarten, it is bordered by Klingelhöfer Strasse, a major boulevard, and the Landwehrkanal, a picturesque waterway. The site is part of the historic diplomatic quarter, close to the embassies of Italy and Japan, and across the street from Walter Gropius' Bauhaus Archives.

The master plan for the site, designed by the office of Machleidt + Stepp as the result of a 1996 competition, mandates a tight urban block structure, a strong street edge, and a continuous eave line. Frequent alleys break up the street wall into smaller increments, while the skewed angles of the alleys and distorted footprints of the building lots echo the site's trapezoidal shape. The center of the site is left void as a public park, surrounded by an equally strong wall of buildings.

View of office buildings along boulevard

TIERGARTEN DREIECK

View along canal: MRY building on left

TIERGARTEN DREIECK

Moore Ruble Yudell was invited to participate in a series of workshops following the master plan design, and was subsequently commissioned to design two buildings, one for luxury condominiums along the canal and another for offices along the boulevard.

The housing block, in its massing and elevations, is classically proportioned, with a strong base, three-story body, and sculpted penthouse. Balanced groups of light steel window bays and balconies organize the facades into a calm order and break the formality of the heavy stone base and plaster walls.

Grouped at the corners of rooms or collected into glassy bays, generous windows bring much daylight into the interiors and provide multiple views to the canal, park, and city beyond. A great variety of unit configurations of different characters is generated by the division of the building footprint into front, center, and rear wings.

Long section

Upper level plan

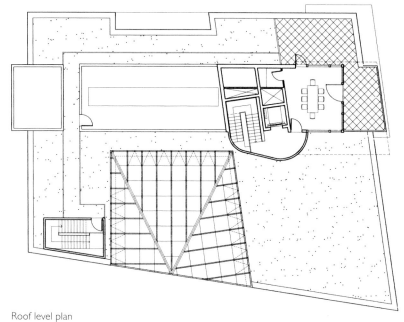

Roof level plan

The office building takes its place along the boulevard as a calm volume, forming a strong street wall as dictated by the master plan. A tall bay above the main entrance acts as a counterpoint to the horizontal banding of the street facade and marks its address along the boulevard. Within the window bands, stainless steel columns rhythmically express the building's structure; cherry wood window frames add warmth and another order of detail to the material palette of gray sandstone and stainless steel.

The narrow building section and generous fenestration fill all office spaces with daylight. The conference rooms are expressed within the bays in the front and rear facades and the penthouse, allowing multiple views of the surroundings. A glazed courtyard opens to the south, providing for a variety of year-round uses.

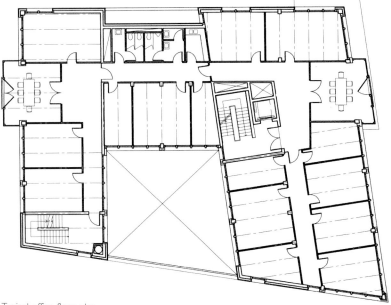

Typical office floor plan

South elevation showing glazed courtyard

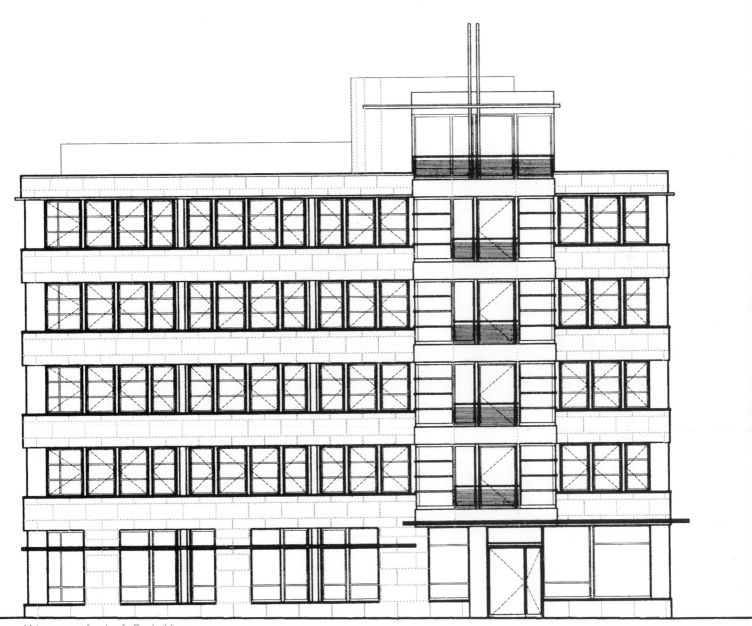

Main entrance facade of office building

Pages From a Berlin Diary

by John Ruble

May 18, 1980

"So … now you are Charles Moore …?"

I looked up nervously to see Rem Koolhaas, with his faintest wry smile, and then glanced back to the place card, which announced Charles Moore's seat at the long dais. That evening, the architects who were about to compete in the *Planungsgutachten Tegeler Hafen* were to present a sample of their work to the public. *Planungsgutachten* in this case meant a paid, invited competition, and at the International Bauausstellung Berlin '84 (IBA) that meant famous architects: Leon Krier from Luxembourg and London, Hermann Hertzberger from Amsterdam, Arata Isozaki from Tokyo, Gunther Behnisch from Stuttgart, and Moore! This was the kind of gathering of world-class talent that Mattias Ungers liked to call the "International Circus," and Rem was one of its emerging high-wire acts.

In 1980 Charles Moore was at the height of his career, and was one of relatively few Americans invited to perform at IBA, despite—or more likely because of—his utterly irreverent view of European Modernism. Charles had found a kindred spirit in Germany in art historian, critic, and theorist Heinrich Klotz. As a passionate, accomplished advocate for architectural humanism, Heinrich had long provided spiritual and intellectual support for Europeans who challenged the Modernist canon, and had invited Charles to events in Berlin and Marburg. With Tegel Harbor, Heinrich was about to become our most important European ally, first by inviting Charles into the competition, and later as a member of the jury. Buzz Yudell had convinced Charles to do the competition at Moore Ruble Yudell, rather than at UCLA's Urban Innovations group, where Charles often did competitions. He was expected at IBA's pre-competition conference, but owing to the triple-booked Moore calendar and my high school German, we decided that I would come to Berlin instead.

The previous day had been my first in West Berlin—a dreamy, round-the-clock tour that began on our site at Tegel Harbor, where a local resident read a long prepared statement in favor of maintaining a small but passionately cared-for playground. It was a *Burgerinitiative*, something the neighbors had made for themselves, which gave the little yard a political edge. The assembled international architects listened patiently until it was time to board a small boat loaded with beer and a luncheon buffet. On a beautiful May afternoon's ride, we drifted across sparkling lakes, down tree-shaded canals, through tiny locks, and past lush shorelines punctuated by glowing yellow-ochre houses in Schinkel's classical-romantic style, which signaled our arrival at Park Glienicke. Here Schinkel, Persius, and landscape architect Joseph Lenne had created one of the world's finest arrangements of building and landscape—a fabled place that I had known only from lectures and books. We stepped off the boat to continue our tour on foot, strolling past the *Schloss*, with its courtyard full of Greek and Roman sculpture, to the famed Casino, a small pavilion flanked by perfectly scaled, minimally detailed pergolas, and out to the *Neugiere*, a little belvedere looking across to Glienicke Bridge,[1] where the princes waited to see who had come from Potsdam to join the party.

1

The bridge was more recently the famous point of exchange for spies from the communist East, but since we couldn't cross it, we spent some hours roaming the park. As the conversation flowed in a mix of languages there came a moment of recognition: walking with Arata Isozaki and Aldo Van Eyck past Lenne's carefully placed tumble of Corinthian capitals—and upturned roots of trees perfectly maintained to look

like Corinthian capitals—I could see that, just as Charles had claimed, modern architecture surely had its beginnings in the early 19th century. For here was the free hand of a modern sensibility at play—modern by virtue of an almost violent freedom of choice, and a reference to the past that made it seem remote and archeological.

As darkness quietly settled, we headed by small buses to the reception that had been organized at Werner Duttmann's unmistakably Modernist suburban home: walls crammed full of modern art, drawings, paintings, graphics, portraits, and photographs of his famously beautiful wife. Here Duttman, a powerful, respected former City Architect, held forth in a round-robin of salon sessions—now a rapt audience of students, now a somewhat more skeptical and tired set of IBA competitors sampling the *wursts*, trying Rote Grütze for the first time, and letting the beer provide sleepy answers to his tireless questions about our plans for Tegel Harbor. At last came the merciful announcement of buses returning us to the hotel, unless of course anyone wanted to check out Berlin's legendary after-hours scene. As it had already been a thirty-six hour day, most of us decided to save that experience for later!

169

The next night in Reinickendorf, I was far too jet-lagged, too anxious about my presentation in Charles' stead, too busy fumbling with my slides and trying desperately to compose a few words in my high school German, to really answer Rem's inquiry. I had known him four years earlier as a spirited studio critic at UCLA, sharp-witted and wonderfully supportive. Now that he was a juror for Tegeler Hafen, I felt we were on opposite sides of a debate just being articulated, and Rem's faint smile meant amusement, not approval.

"We're partners," I offered, without elaboration; I had to save what little wit I had for the show. I could hardly have imagined that several months later we would win the Tegel Competition—with Heinrich Klotz's support, and over Rem's strenuous objections.

March 8, 1981

"Important people are always late."

Walter Stepp was trying to calm me down as we sloshed our way through traffic and wet snow to the city offices on Wurttembergische Strasse. In those days Walter worked for IBA as our project manager, and had been taking me on a two-day, packed agenda. Bouncing from one agency to another, we tried to nail down procedures and contracts for different parts of the Tegel Harbor plan: the housing, public library, extended harbor, and waterfront promenade were all to be produced and paid for by different entities, and the miracle from my point of view was that they were all "stepping up to the plate." Tales of competitions that went nowhere were common in Germany, but the magic letters I, B and A opened doors and bank accounts all over town for this one—it seemed indeed that we were going to build ourselves a waterfront!

But being late for the meetings jangled my jet-lagged nerves and hobbled my German. The whole week had started badly. Thomas Nagel, our project manager, and I had rushed breathlessly into a classic Berlin meeting right off the plane, one hour late, and here is what we saw: a six-meter long table complete with white tablecloth was thickly strewn with dishes of pastry accompanied by bowls of whipped cream, pots and cups of coffee, bottles of very gassy water, and ashtrays, lots of ashtrays. Both sides of the table were lined with mostly bearded men in sweaters and suits, each row disappearing into the dense

PAGES FROM A BERLIN DIARY BY JOHN RUBLE

cloud of cigarette and cigar smoke. At the far end, I could just make out the white-shirted mass of Ruths, Senior, patriarch and director of the infamous Ingenieur Bureau Ruths, and a central figure in Berlin's so-called Building Mafia, his voice booming: "And where is Doctor Moore this morning … ?!?"

Charles wasn't due for two more days, and stand-in Ruble was not well received. Neither were the revisions to the plans we had brought—unenthusiastic compromises to attempt compliance with German codes— particularly the dreaded Abstandsflächen, the complex requirements for setback between buildings which have ruined many a foreign architect's concept. It was decided that we would stay in Berlin as long as necessary to make the work good again. One doesn't argue with Ruths, Senior!

Two days later, after some confusing but successful meetings with the City, Walter dropped me at our temporary offices— donated space in the old Zeiss Optik factory—where an entire team of German friends had come to our rescue. There were Maya Reiner and Jörg Weber from Munich, who both had attended Berkeley and worked

with Bill Turnbull there. Maya had become indispensable to me as translator and advisor in the meetings, and had assembled a bright, hard-working crew for the week, including two other friends, Kai and Kristiane Haag from Stuttgart, also via Berkeley where Kai worked with Joe Esherick. In other words, we had a ready-made Bay Area team, quite conversant with the work and philosophy of the whole Moore family!

By then Charles had arrived and was taking a nap on a rug. Kai was fascinated but concerned: "At last I have the chance to work with this great man, and he's sleeping on the floor!" But work we did, producing in just three intensive days and nights an entirely new presentation, complete with a new design by Charles for the recreation island, and a splendid ink-line perspective of the harbor by Maya.[2] It has always moved me, this capacity of my German friends and colleagues for inspired, concentrated work; the ability to set to it and not look up until the job is done, and done beautifully. Maya's team made just that sort of effort for us at a time when we had to prove ourselves, and they did so entirely out of a love of architecture.

2

"It's looking very big … and very colorful!"
Jan Wehberg, with a sweep of an arm and an impish grin, filled me in as we rode with Cornelia Müller to Tegel Harbor on a beautiful spring afternoon, just as their landscape for the project was being completed. Thomas Nagel and I had had two years of intensive travel to attend the project through documents and construction. Finally we were about to see the project complete with finishes, color, and residents. Jan's description allowed me to wonder whether the end result was, perhaps, a bit too colorful?

It would be hard to overstate how important the color design is to the housing at Tegel. Apart from its zinc roof, the entire exterior is either plaster or paint. For our colorist, Tina Beebe, it was an early opportunity to apply to a large project the ideas that she and Charles Moore had explored for years on houses. After initial color studies on our models, Tina had worked for weeks with the plaster contractor to produce large-scale

elevations detailing every color surface. Our developer, Dietmar Otremba, was a bit put off by the sheer amount of color and detail but, to his credit, committed entirely to realizing the design.

The palette both articulates and unifies: constant colors for windows and concrete pilasters play across a shifting, almost musical scale of wall colors, giving this mid-rise wall of housing the visual quality of an Italian hill town. In fact, Berlin's classical-romantic period of building, the early 19th century works that had interested us as the context for Tegel, is very much a love affair with Italian light and color, subtly adjusted for the mid-European climate. As we discovered, Tina had hit all the right notes: the creams, ochres and roses coaxed every bit of warmth from the slanting light of early March. In the summer you could almost feel them vibrate in the lush, watery setting.[3]

Tegel's lyrical, narrative quality comes equally from the landscape design. Cornelia and Jan immediately understood the transitional nature of the urban planning: villas-on-parade along the edge of the town open processional spaces to the waterfront, where the much larger walls of housing bend and move, animated by the sensuous panorama of lakes

3

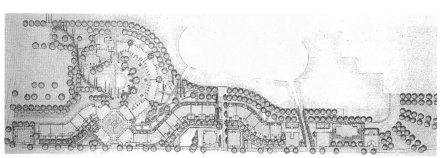

4

and forests beyond.[4] The grandly gated entry courtyard at the street is playfully "paved" with a panel of lawn and floating squares of polished granite, which Cornelia demonstrates—hopping from square to square—as we stroll through. The big tiles are later recalled in the smaller granite forms of Platonic cubes and spheres that emerge unexpectedly along paths and edges. I remembered Lenne's recursive forms at Glienicke, the upturned roots reappearing as Corinthian capitals.

Behind the entry courtyard is a large open-sided garden—we called it the Commons— where a narrow walk marks an axis through to the water. But equally, one is drawn sideways to the waterfront promenade by a rippling "curtain" of poplars along a small, rocky rill. Children play in the rill: the sandy bottom and a water tap make it irresistible. Like all great landscape, the garden design at Tegel operates in the realm of desire and delight. This quality, more than any other, suggests what the art of landscape can provide as an ally in making places: whatever functional problems have been solved—and there are many—we are blissfully unaware of them. We are invited to enjoy the richness of a place, and delight in what has been made entirely, it seems, for our pleasure. That Jan

and Cornelia have been able to negotiate this kind of experience into what are, after all, social housing projects, has certainly earned them a place in Berlin's history of design.

January 21, 1991

"I've always said that housing is the hardest thing to design well!"
Buzz Yudell and I nodded sympathetically as Dieter Graalfs addressed an unusual gathering of architects at the Cecilienhof in Potsdam. As our developer client, and an architect himself by training, he often felt moved to lecture to us.

Dieter is a free-market humanist. At every opportunity he argues for architecture and planning that is both humanistic and pragmatic: not interested in ideal conceptions of order and form, but devoted to the needs of people—an architecture to satisfy the *Bauch* (the belly) if not the mind. He personifies our vision of an enlightened German capitalist: despite the millions he and his partners have made, Dieter builds social housing as if he were going to live there himself.

His firm, Groth + Graalfs, had called the architects together for a collaboration that was unprecedented in Germany: a workshop/ competition. One American and five

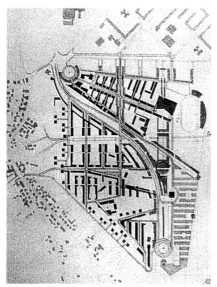

5

6

European architects were to present, debate, and exchange ideas for Kirchsteigfeld, a large mixed-use development near Potsdam, after which the best design would form the basis for a town plan that we all would build together.

It had been just three years since our Tegel Harbor housing was completed, but in that time the world had changed: Berlin was no longer an island! Almost before the Wall came down, Western developers were chasing land deals in the East, getting into position for the inevitable redevelopment of East Berlin, Brandenburg, Leipzig, and Dresden. Groth + Graalfs had two of the largest areas: Kirchsteigfeld in Potsdam and Karow Nord in Berlin Weissensee, undeveloped sites for almost 50,000 inhabitants. With the planning of a new Berlin there was money, but also history, to be made.

The workshop revealed a broad range of ideas about community planning, from Rob Krier's medieval town, with its narrow streets and tightly formed piazzas, to Romaldo Burelli's post-industrial *Siedlung*—a rich collage of building types and patterns held together by a stunning sweep of open space, a hybrid "urban arroyo," combining park, boulevard, streetcar, shops, schools, and a church.[5]

As the discussion got into full swing, Burelli elaborated his ideas in heavily Italian-accented German, his powerful hands chopping the air to describe a rhythm of alleys and courtyards, grabbing a pocket of space above our heads and dragging it across the room to carve that grand arroyo. For the first time in the meeting, Buzz—who had just started German lessons himself—understood the language perfectly![6]

Rob Krier, not to be outdone, mounted chair and used his ample midsection to pin his large, colorful plans to the wall.[7] Soon Rob had conjured up a vision of life in the new Kirchsteigfeld that sounded an awful lot like 17th century Vienna, as he demonstrated how "Oma" (Grandma) would easily find her way to the market "for a bucket of coal." Dieter Graalfs looked on with satisfaction as the Berlin Modernists in the group lit cigarettes, stared at the table, and slowly shook their heads.

Our own plan[8] synthesized two opposing traditions in modern German housing: the *Siedlung*, with its orderly attention to orientation, open space, and sunlight; and the *Vorstadt*, the typical turn-of-the century district at the edge of Berlin, with its more developed qualities of hierarchy and place.

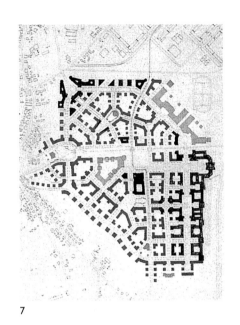

7

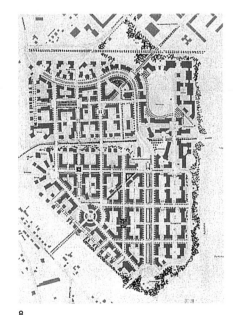

8

A basic organization of rectangular blocks was oriented with the long dimension north–south, letting winter light into streets and courtyards, which were defined with a variety of building types. Smaller villas and gaps punctuated the solid street walls, allowing public and semi-public open spaces to form a continuous network of green. This pedestrian network led to the Hirten Graben, a linear park along a small creek, and to the town center.

Dieter drew a series of points, largely from our plan, and strongly urged the workshop to move in that direction, which they did—especially Rob Krier and his partner Christoph Kohl, whose revised design stole the show at the next meeting. We were invited to Vienna to work together on their winning plan, after which the first phase of about 600 units would be divided among the competitors.

A few months later, the workshop architects met again to fit models of their respective pieces together, using Krier & Kohl's urban plan and guidelines. Each architect had about ten small buildings, corresponding to a variety of conditions and types—a corner *Haus* with a tower, a mid-block *Haus* with bay windows, and a freestanding Villa—all three to four stories high with pitched roofs and balconies.

It was immediately evident that the overall quality of accumulation was far more interesting than anyone's particular *Haus*. The decisions of each architect within the whole are strengthened, rather than contradicted, by the accidental relationship to neighboring designs.

One can criticize many things—perhaps the color scheme is a bit too insistent, and there is a kind of sweetness which would only trouble an architect or critic—but we would argue that Kirchsteigfeld captures much of the visual interest of an urban district developed over time. Even the larger, more repetitive commercial center buildings cannot dominate the scale and rhythm of a cumulative place. Whether we call it a town or a housing development, this is an extraordinary setting for community, and more so for having been conceived and built in only six years.

April 7, 1995

"The square, the circle, the octagon—each of these places had its own quite distinctive figure …"

Hans Stimmann, the *Senatsbaudirektor* of Berlin, led a group of American architects on a tour of Berlin's historic ground plan, using an aerial photograph from the 1930s. The architects had been chosen carefully by the U.S. Department of State to take part in a competition for the design of the new American Embassy in Berlin. All had noted, distinguished practices, and some, like Robert Venturi, were legendary.

They had been selected in a nationwide search and had all made the cut, to some extent because their work showed a deep interest in the specifics of places—especially historic urban centers. As he outlined the basic aims of his department—to reconstruct the historic plan of the city using contemporary architecture—Stimmann seemed not to realize that he was preaching to the choir. But while the Americans there accepted implicitly the value of a historic city plan, the issue was deeply divisive for Berliners.

Since the end of World War II, one of the great cultural debates in Berlin has been whether to rebuild the city—not how, but whether to do so at all. Immediately following the war, many Berliners turned on what little was left of their historic city and savagely attacked it, stripping the damaged details of 18th and 19th century buildings, and demolishing many more, for economic or ideological reasons. Post-war architects preferred Modern buildings floating in the resulting open space—idealized in a mid-1950s plan by Hans Scharoun—and building sites were purposely left vacant all over town.

The significance was double-edged: for many Berliners, the emptiness suggested a future free of the past, while for others, empty lots became an important reminder of the war and all that had led up to it.

As the West prospered, restoration became more fashionable, while in the East it remained monetarily if not politically out of the question: when Schinkel's Schauspielhaus was restored for the 1987 bicentennial, the work was paid for by West Germany. West Berlin's International Bauaustellung Berlin '87 was fully devoted to urban restoration, both with new construction and adaptive reuse. Yet interestingly, the directors split into two quite antagonistic camps—new projects and reconstruction—whose agendas were never joined in any of IBA's many works. Even in the materialistic 1980s, rebuilding stirred deep political conflicts.

Since reunification, this question has heated up and city policy has reflected a succession of viewpoints on the issue. Almost as soon as the Wall came down, a series of public forums was held to allow open discussion. It was during this time that City Architect Hans Stimmann promoted the policy known as "critical reconstruction"—the restoration of the city's pre-war patterns of buildings, streets, and squares—all using modern architecture bounded by strict guidelines. For taking this relatively clear, post-reconstruction stand, Stimmann became a favorite villain in Berlin's architecture scene.

It was under this set of policies and urban design philosophy that the State Department undertook the 1995 design competition for its new Berlin Embassy. The site at the southwest corner of Pariser Platz[9], where the pre-war American Embassy once stood, was almost shoulder to shoulder with the Brandenburger Tor, Germany's most famous landmark, and proudest symbol of its national heritage.

As historic sites go, Pariser Platz was a very curious place indeed. Empty, except for the Brandenburg Gate, it had become a loose, open-air market for nested Russian dolls and old military insignia from the German Democratic Republic. Tourists who came to see the Gate might also wander across the grass to view a small plaque at Number Two Pariser Platz, announcing the future American Embassy. That address is now, somewhat famously, the only one on the Platz that is still vacant, as a new phase of the city's development rises up all around it.

After the briefing with Stimmann we toured the site, which seemed large, and studied the Gate, which was … not very large. Conceived

9

and built in the 1780s, the Gate has been a powerful form in the gentler context of 18th century Friedrichstadt. The buildings to either side were modest in scale, and formed solid walls all around Pariser Platz, allowing the Gate to have its relative monumentality and supporting its function as a portal into the city. Urban design guidelines for the district sought to recreate these conditions, and so did we, as we began designing our proposal for the embassy.

The scale of the embassy is for us one of the most critical objectives of its design. We made a decision that day of the tour that the embassy's symbolic messages—the dynamic, pluralist American democracy, the presence of a vigilant world power—would all find expression within its place as part of a larger whole. Indeed, the political point of building on the Pariser Platz site is to declare our alliance in the rebirth of Berlin as a democratic capital. To do so meant that, as Charles Moore would have said, you had to "get it right."

Of course, we urgently wanted to win. Our work in Berlin all started with a competition, and led to many years of working around the periphery, with several unsuccessful competitions in the center. But the opportunity to build in the historic core of the capital has been, and still is, worth waiting for.

Los Angeles, 1999

PROJECT

UNITED STATES EMBASSY

UNITED STATES EMBASSY

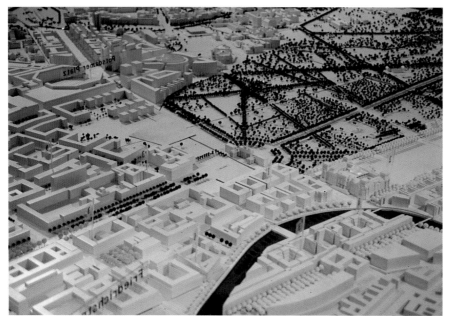

Berlin city model with Pariser Platz in center

The new U.S. Embassy in Berlin occupies a focal position at the symbolic and political center of the reunified Germany. In this exceptional place and time, Moore Ruble Yudell's 1996 competition-winning design seeks to reflect both American values and a respect for the people and culture of Germany.

As a background as well as a partner for the Brandenburg Gate, the new embassy maintains a respectful yet spirited dialogue with its surroundings, architecturally playing out the relationship between the two governments. By day and night, the copper and glass lantern of the rooftop State Room Pavilion serves as a beacon on the city skyline, signaling the American presence and the democratic values shared by the two countries.

Proposed embassy seen across Brandenburg Gate

UNITED STATES EMBASSY

Opposite: Main entry on Pariser Platz

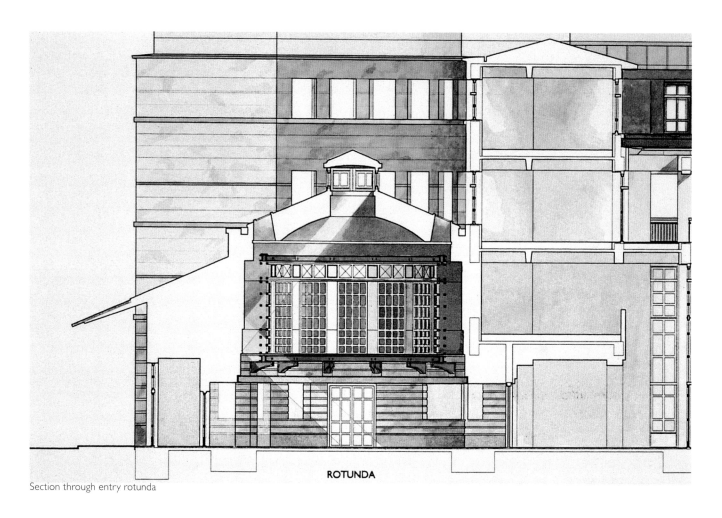

Section through entry rotunda

Model view from Pariser Platz

UNITED STATES EMBASSY

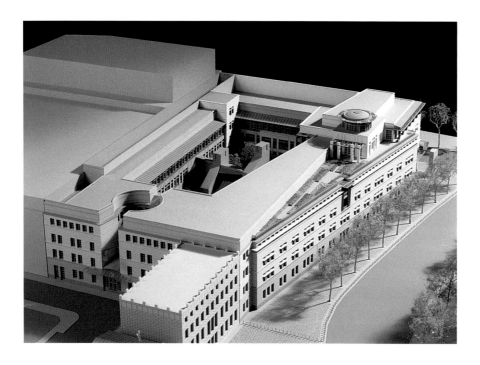

Marking the Pariser Platz entry, a gently curved glass canopy evokes the American flag, which flies just above it. The facade parts at its center to reveal the civic dome of the entry rotunda and to allow the southern sun to stream in, illuminating the flag and extending the space of the public *platz* into the space of the embassy.

Given its extraordinary location, the new embassy is in a prime position to serve the business of state. Special features, such as the ground floor conference and exhibition center, support a variety of cultural and commercial purposes.

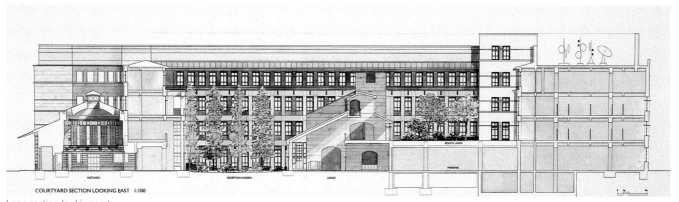

COURTYARD SECTION LOOKING EAST 1:100

Long section looking east

UNITED STATES EMBASSY

The Chancery's elegant State Room, with spectacular views of the Reichstag, accommodates luncheons and other high-level receptions just a short walk from the new government center. The greening of the rooftop—a focal point of the embassy's urban design—allows a parterre garden to act as foreground for the Gate and its Quadriga sculpture.

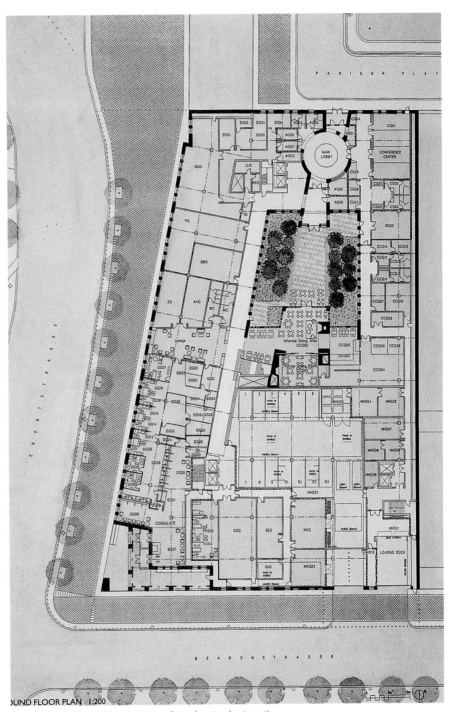

Ground floor plan: embassy entrance through rotunda at north facing Pariser Platz; consulate entrance at southwest corner facing boulevard; north court is at grade, south lawn above parking.

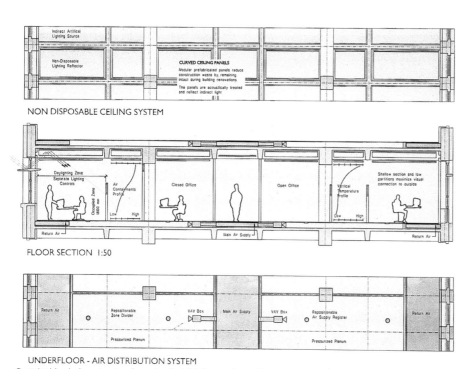

NON DISPOSABLE CEILING SYSTEM

FLOOR SECTION 1:50

UNDERFLOOR - AIR DISTRIBUTION SYSTEM

Sustainable design: structural, mechanical, lighting, and partition systems are integrated

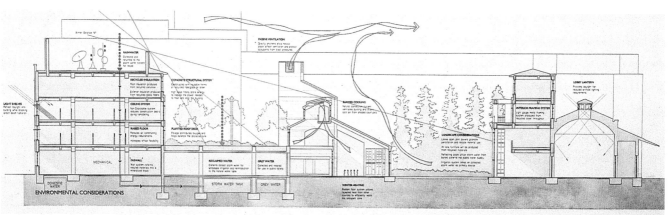

Long section showing environmental strategies: solar angles, gray water recycling, use of recycled building materials, integrated building systems

The Chancery is planned around a courtyard which offers the advantage of combining a large area of contiguous floorspace for maximum flexibility with relatively narrow building depths, which enhance natural daylighting for the interior. To encourage cooperation and interaction, the central courtyard is bridged by walkways at each level leading to the Lodge—a shared dining and conference center set within the interior gardens. Between the two gardens and at the intersection of the main circulation paths, the Lodge is a focus for the embassy community. Its form and scale recall both the iconic importance of the American house and the grand federal legacy of our national parks.

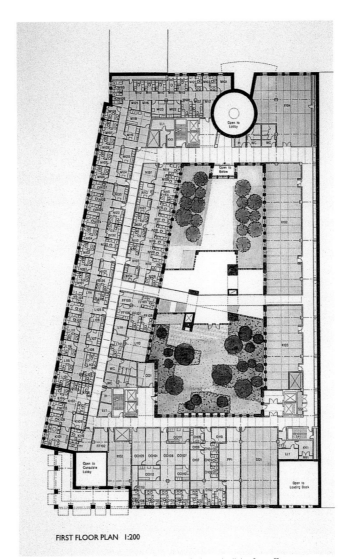

FIRST FLOOR PLAN 1:200

Typical floor plan: courtyard scheme maximizes daylight for offices

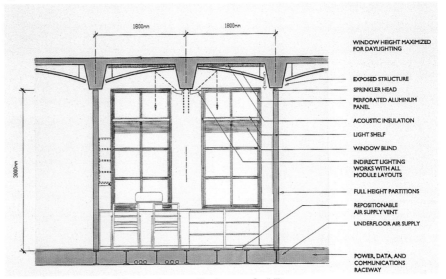

Typical office section: raised floor and open ceiling increase flexibility

187

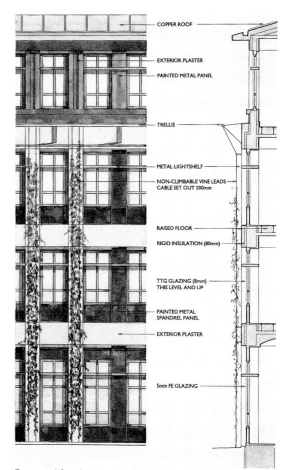

COPPER ROOF

EXTERIOR PLASTER
PAINTED METAL PANEL

TRELLIS

METAL LIGHTSHELF
NON-CLIMBABLE VINE LEADS
CABLE SET OUT 200mm

RAISED FLOOR
RIGID INSULATION (80mm)

TTG GLAZING (8mm)
THIS LEVEL AND UP

PAINTED METAL
SPANDREL PANEL

EXTERIOR PLASTER

5min FE GLAZING

Courtyard facade: stucco and metal panels. Vertical greening
with vines adds to courtyard landscape and rooftop garden
to improve climate

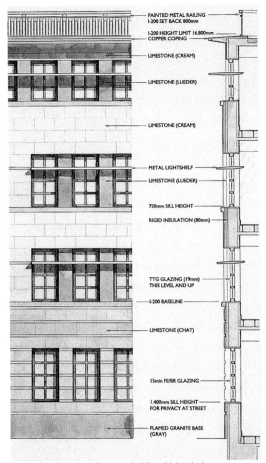

Street facade: natural stone cladding. Light shelves are
for solar control

Cross-section looking at Lodge

The embassy's space planning also responds to the need for future change. Concentrating most of the Chancery program on just four floors facilitates interaction and allows the staff maximum opportunity for collaboration. A careful analysis of the Chancery program led Moore Ruble Yudell to simplify the number of office types and sizes: when assignments change, personnel can move easily and more walls can stay put. The structural bay and modular planning combine with a raised floor system to allow reorganization without the waste of disposable interior finishes, and provide the entire embassy facility with a new standard of quality, economy, and flexibility.

An integrated systems approach to the Chancery building emphasizes resource and energy conservation. Cooling and ventilation take maximum advantage of outside air for nighttime pre-cooling and reduced energy consumption. Natural and artificial lighting are optimally tuned to provide an efficient and enjoyable working environment.

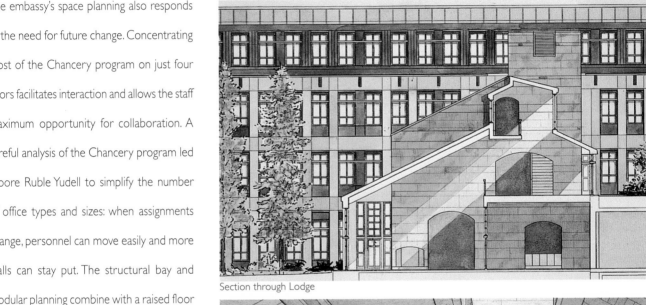
Section through Lodge

Interior of Lodge

Opposite: view of north courtyard and Lodge

View from southwest

UNITED STATES EMBASSY

Elevation and model of southwest corner: consular entrance
at street, Ambassador's Suite and State Room at roof

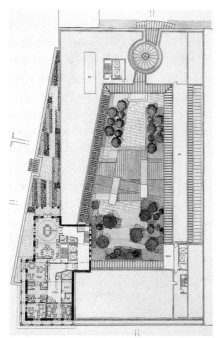

Roof level plan with Ambassador's Suite
and State Room, and rooftop garden

The lantern in dialogue with the Quadriga

State Room with lantern

Opposite: View from State Room across rooftop
garden to Brandenburg Gate and Reichstag beyond

UNITED STATES EMBASSY

John Ruble,
FAIA

Education

Master of Architecture, University of California, Los Angeles, School of Architecture and Urban Planning, 1976

Bachelor of Architecture, University of Virginia, 1969

Teaching Experience

Lecturer, University of California, Los Angeles, School of Architecture and Urban Planning, 1981 to 1992

Visiting Lecturer, Cornell University, 1976

Teaching Associate, University of California, Los Angeles, School of Architecture and Urban Planning, 1975

Professional Experience

Principal, Moore Ruble Yudell, Santa Monica, California, 1977 to present

Consultant, Direct Energy Corporation, Irvine, California (solar heating and cooling development grant, U.S. Department of Energy), 1977 to 1978

Associated with Charles W. Moore, Los Angeles, 1976 to 1977

Project Manager, Urban Innovations Group, Los Angeles, 1976 to 1977

Associated with O.M. Ungers, Ithaca, New York, 1976

Designer, Uniplan, Princeton, New Jersey, 1971 to 1975

Urban Designer, Peace Corps, Tunisia Kasserine Bureau d'Urbanisme, Ministre de Tourisme et l'Amenagement du Territoire, 1969 to 1970

Selected Published Writing

"Communities of Purpose." In *Campus and Community: Moore Ruble Yudell Architecture & Planning*, by Oscar Riera Ojeda, James Mary O'Connor, and Wendy Kohn. Rockport, MA: Rockport Publishers, 1997.

"The Field Trip." In *Moore Ruble Yudell*, edited by James Steele. London: Academy Editions, 1993.

Henry Nielebock. "John Ruble, MRY." In *Jahrbuch 2*. Berlin: Sabine Konopka Publisher, 1987.

"Interview with John Ruble." *Veery Magazine* (December 1996).

Distinction/Service

College of Fellows, American Institute of Architects, 1997

Lecture, Lawrence Technological University, Southfield, Michigan, 1993

"Dualities," lecture with Buzz Yudell, College of Environmental Design, University of California, Berkeley, 1993

Rancho Mirage Civic Center Competition Jury, 1992

Orange County AIA Design Awards Jury, 1991

Dean's Award for Distinguished Service, UCLA School of Architecture and Urban Planning, 1976

Buzz Yudell,
FAIA

Education

Master of Architecture, Yale School of Architecture, 1973

Bachelor of Arts cum laude, Yale College, 1969

Teaching Experience

Adjunct Professor, University of California, Los Angeles, School of Architecture and Urban Planning, 1977 to present

Visiting Critic, Technical University of Nova Scotia, Halifax School of Architecture, 1983

Visiting Critic, University of Texas at Austin, School of Architecture, 1981

Visiting Critic in Architectural Design, Yale School of Architecture, 1972 to 1976

Professional Experience

Principal, Moore Ruble Yudell, Santa Monica, California, 1977 to present

Designer/Project Manager, Charles Moore Architect, Los Angeles, California, 1976 to 1977

Project Manager, Urban Innovations Group, Los Angeles, California, 1976 to 1977

Principal, General Eclectic, New Haven, Connecticut, 1974 to 1976

Evans Wollen Architects, Hotchkiss, Connecticut (site office), 1973

Charles W. Moore Associates/Moore Grover Harper, Essex, Connecticut, 1972 to 1973

Selected Published Writing

"Buildings that Merge and Mark, Streets that Order and Dance." *Places* (vol. II, no. 3, Winter 1998).

"The Shape of Community." In *Campus and Community: Moore Ruble Yudell Architecture & Planning* by Oscar Riera Ojeda, James Mary O'Connor, and Wendy Kohn. Rockport, MA: Rockport Publishers, 1997.

"Houses: Shelter, Dreams and Community." In *Moore Ruble Yudell: Houses & Housing.* AIA Press, 1994.

"Collisions of the Ideal and the Uncertain." *Space Design* (no. 266, November 1986).

"Moore in Progress." *Global Architecture* (Tokyo, no. 7, 1980).

"Body Movement." In *Body, Memory and Architecture.* New Haven and London: Yale Press, 1977. (Contributor with Charles W. Moore and Kent Bloomer.)

Distinction/Service

College of Fellows, American Institute of Architects, 1996

"Late Entries to the Tribune Competition," drawing exhibited in Centre Pompidou, Paris; St. Louis Art Museum; Museum of Contemporary Art, Chicago, 1977

Alpha Rho Chi Medal, Yale School of Architecture, 1972

Fellow, Branford College, Yale University

Second Prize, Competition for Cultural Center for Plateau Beaubourg, with Moshe Safdie, Architect, 1971

Chronological
List of
Projects

Rodes House
Los Angeles, California
1977–1979

St. Matthew's Episcopal Church
Pacific Palisades, California
1979–1983

Kwee House
Singapore
1980–1985

Tegel Harbor Housing
Berlin, Germany
Competition 1980
Phase I 1981–1988
Phase II 1995–present

Tegel Harbor Villa
Berlin, Germany
1985–1989

Humboldt Bibliothek
Berlin, Germany
1984–1988

Parador Hotel
San Juan Capistrano, California
1982 (project)

Marine Street House
Santa Monica, California
1981–1983

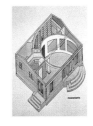 

San Antonio Art Institute
San Antonio, Texas
1982–1989

St. Louis Art Museum
West Wing Renovation and New
Decorative Arts Galleries
St. Louis, Missouri
1983–1987

Carousel Park
Santa Monica Pier, Santa Monica, California
Competition 1984
1984–1987

Inman House
Atlanta, Georgia
1984–1987

Plaza Las Fuentes
Pasadena, California
Phase I 1983–1989

Bel Air Presbyterian Church
Los Angeles, California
1984–1993

University of Oregon Science Complex
Eugene, Oregon
1985–1989

Anawalt House
Malibu, California
1985–1988

The Peter Boxenbaum Arts Education Center,
Crossroads School
Santa Monica, California
1986–1988

Nativity Catholic Church
Rancho Santa Fe, California
1985–1989

UCSD Cellular and Molecular Medicine, East and West Wings
University of California, San Diego, California
1986–1989, 1991–1995

First Church of Christ, Scientist
Glendale, California
1986–1989

Playa Vista Master Plan
Los Angeles, California
1987–present

Yudell/Beebe House
Malibu, California
1987–1989

Walter A. Haas School of Business
University of California, Berkeley, California
1987–1995

Powell Library Renovation and Addition
University of California, Los Angeles, California
1988–1996

Nishiokamoto Housing
Kobe, Japan
Phases I & II 1988–1992
Phase III 1994–1996

Potatisåkern Housing
Malmö, Sweden
Phase I & II 1988–1996
Phase III 1997–present

California Center for the Arts
Escondido, California
1987–1994

University of Washington Chemistry Building
Seattle, Washington
1988–1995

Malibu Housing
Malibu, California
1988 (project)

Bolle Center
Berlin, Germany
1990 (project)

Villa Superba
Venice, California
1990–1993

Schetter House
Pacific Palisades, California
1991–1996

Friedrichstadt Passagen
Berlin, Germany
1991 (project)

University of Washington
Tacoma Campus Master Plan
Tacoma, Washington
Phase I 1991–1998
Phase II 1998–present

Berliner Strasse Housing
Potsdam, Germany
1991–1998

Kirchsteigfeld Master Plan and Housing
Berlin, Germany
Competition 1992
1993–1998

Peek & Cloppenburg Department Store
Berlin, Germany
1992 (project)

Peek & Cloppenburg Department Store
Leipzig, Germany
Competition 1992
1992–1994

CHRONOLOGICAL LIST OF PROJECTS

Dong-Hwa National University Master Plan
Hwa-Lien, Taiwan
Competition 1992
1992–present

Avery House
California Institute of Technology, Pasadena, California
Competition 1992
1992–1996

Konstancin Housing
Warsaw, Poland
1993–1996 (project)

The Hugh and Hazel Darling Law Library Addition
University of California, Los Angeles, California
1992–1998

Walrod Residence
Berkeley, California
1992–1994

Karow Nord Master Plan & Housing
Weissensee, Germany
Competition 1992
1992–1999

Sherman M. Fairchild Library of Engineering and Applied Science
California Institute of Technology, Pasadena, California
1993–1998

Göttingen Master Plan
Göttingen, Germany
1993–present

Kao-Shiung Institute of Technology
Campus Master Plan Design
Kao-Shiung, Taiwan
1993 (project)

Maryland Center for Performing Arts
University of Maryland, College Park, Maryland
Competition 1994
1994–present

Shanghai Grand Theatre
Shanghai, People's Republic of China
1994 (project)

Uludag Ski Resort
Bursa, Turkey
1995–present

United States Embassy
Berlin, Germany
Competition 1995
1995–present

House in Mustique
French Virgin Islands
1996–1997 (project)

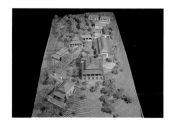

Percival/Westbrook House
Newport Coast, California
1995–1998

Elizabeth Moore House
Orinda, California
1996–1998

Wasserstein House
Santa Barbara, California
1994–present

Shmuger/Hamagami House
Los Angeles, California
1995–1999

Yorkin House
Malibu, California
1996–1999

Gilbert Remodel
Los Angeles, California
1996–1998

Graalfs House
Berlin, Germany
1996–1999

Cayman Shores Development
Grand Cayman, Cayman Islands
1996–present

Regatta Wharf Housing/Sydney Harbour
Sydney, Australia
1996–present

United States Courthouse
Fresno, California
1996–present

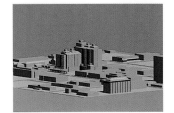

Tiergarten Dreieck Housing
Berlin, Germany
1996–2000

Tiergarten Dreieck Offices
Berlin, Germany
1996–2000

San Rafael Student Housing
University of California, Santa Barbara, California
1997–present

Göttingen Office Building
Göttingen, Germany
1997–1999

Nautilus Condominiums
Yesilyurt, Turkey
1997–present

Miramar Villas
Guzelce, Turkey
1997–present

Baas/Walrod House
Sea Ranch, California
1997–present

Interdisciplinary Sciences Building
University of California, Santa Cruz, California
1997–present

Fairmont Towers Hotel
San Jose, California
1997–present

Playa Vista Office Campus
Los Angeles, California
1997–present

Congregation Beth El
Berkeley, California
1997–present

Sloan School of Business
Massachusetts Institute of Technology, Massachusetts
1998 (project)

Disney Imagineering Master Plan
Glendale, California
1998–present

Tutt Science Center
Colorado College, Colorado
1998–present

House for the Next Millennium
House Beautiful Magazine
1998 (project)

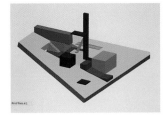

Selected Firm
Awards and
Exhibitions

Awards

Honor Award for Urban Design
American Institute of Architects
Tacoma Campus Master Plan & Phase I,
University of Washington
1999

Merit Award
California Council, American Institute of
Architects
Tacoma Campus Master Plan
University of Washington
1999

Honor Award
American Institute of Architects
Powell Library Renovation and Addition,
University of California, Los Angeles
1998

AIA/ALA Library Buildings Award
American Institute of Architects/American
Library Association
Powell Library Renovation and Addition,
University of California, Los Angeles
1997

Los Angeles Business Council Award
Powell Library Renovation and Addition,
University of California, Los Angeles
1997

Los Angeles Conservancy Award
Powell Library Renovation and Addition,
University of California, Los Angeles
1997

California Governor's Historic Preservation
Award
Powell Library Renovation and Addition,
Los Angeles, California
1996

First Prize, National Design Competition
United States Department of State
United States Embassy in Berlin
1996

IIDA Edwin F. Guth Award for Interior
Lighting Design
California Center for the Arts, Escondido
1996

Lumen West Award for Lighting Design
California Center for the Arts, Escondido
1996

Winner Architectural Category
American Concrete Institute
Walter A. Haas School of Business,
Berkeley, California
1995

Merit Award
United States Institute for Theater
Technology
California Center for the Arts, Escondido
1995

Bronze Award for Architectural Excellence
Stucco Manufacturers Association
California Center for the Arts, Escondido
1995

Citation
American Association of School
Administrators
Walter A. Haas School of Business,
Berkeley, California
1994

Concrete Masonry Design Award
Cellular and Molecular Medicine, West
Wing
University of California, San Diego
1994

Interiors Award
American Institute of Architects
Nativity Catholic Church
1993

Interior Award
Interiors Magazine
Nativity Catholic Church
1992

Firm of the Year Award
California Council, American Institute of
Architects
1992

Urban Design Award
California Council, American Institute of
Architects
Plaza Las Fuentes, Pasadena
1992

First Place, People's Choice Awards
Southwestern Oregon Chapter, American
Institute of Architects
University of Oregon Science Complex
1992

Citation Winner
Southwestern Oregon Chapter, American
Institute of Architects
University of Oregon Science Complex
1992

Honor Award
California Council, American Institute of
Architects
Yudell/Beebe House, Malibu
1992

Award of Merit
AIA/*Sunset* Magazine Western Home
Awards
Yudell/Beebe House, Malibu
1991–1992

Library Building Award
American Institute of Architects/American
Library Association
Humboldt Bibliothek
1991

Honor Award
San Diego Chapter, American Institute of
Architects
Nativity Catholic Church
1991

Honor Award
American Wood Council
First Church of Christ Scientist, Glendale,
California
1991

Honor Award
California Council, American Institute of
Architects
First Church of Christ, Scientist, Glendale,
California
1991

Award
American Institute of Architects/American
Library Association
Humboldt Bibliothek
1990

Honor Award
Los Angeles Chapter, American Institute of
Architects
Humboldt Bibliothek
1990

Merit Award
California Council, American Institute of
Architects
House on Point Dume
1989

Honor Award
American Institute of Architects
Tegel Harbor Housing
1988

Honor Award
California Council, American Institute of
Architects
Tegel Harbor Housing
1988

Honor Award
California Council, American Institute of
Architects
Carousel Park
1988

Building a Better Future Honor Award
State of California Department of
Rehabilitation Architectural Design Awards
Program
Carousel Park
1987

Mayor's Commendation
City of Santa Monica
Carousel Park
October 1987

Excellence on the Waterfront Honor
Award
Carousel Park
Waterfront Center
1987

Honor Award
American Institute of Architects
St. Matthew's Episcopal Church
1984

Merit Award
California Council, American Institute of
Architects
St. Matthew's Episcopal Church
1984

Merit Award
Los Angeles Chapter, American Institute of
Architects
St. Matthew's Episcopal Church
1984

House of the Year
Architectural Record
Rodes House
1981

First Prize
Santa Monica Pier Design Charrette
1981

First Prize
Housing, Recreational and Cultural Center
Tegel Harbor International Design
Competition, West Berlin
1980

Exhibitions

"Urban Revisions," Museum of
Contemporary Art, Los Angeles, 1994

"Transitions: Moore Ruble Yudell Works in
Progress," UCLA School of Architecture
Gallery, 1994

"Der Revision der Moderne Postmodern,
Architecture 1960–1980," Deutschen
Architeckturmuseum, Frankfurt, West
Germany, 1984

"Das Abenteuer der Ideen," National
Galerie, Berlin, West Germany, 1984

"Contemporary Views of the House,"
Mandeville Gallery, University of California
San Diego, 1983

"The California Condition," La Jolla Museum
of Contemporary Art, 1982

Exhibition, Max Protetch Gallery, NYC
St. Matthew's Episcopal Church
1980

Selected
Published Work

Listed in reverse chronological order.

Books

Ojeda, Oscar Riera, James Mary O'Connor, and Wendy Kohn. *Campus & Community: Moore Ruble Yudell Architecture & Planning.* Rockport, MA: Rockport Publishers, 1997.

Ojeda, Oscar Riera and Lucas H. Guerra. *Moore Ruble Yudell: Houses and Housing.* Washington, D.C.: AIA Press, 1994.

Steele, James (ed.). *Moore Ruble Yudell.* London: Academy Editions, 1993.

Moore Ruble Yudell 1979–1992. A+U special issue. Tokyo: A+U Publishing Co., Ltd., August 1992.

Johnson, Eugene J. (ed.). *Charles Moore: Buildings and Projects 1949–1986.* New York: Rizzoli, 1986. (St. Matthew's Episcopal Church; Tegel Harbor Housing; Humboldt Library; San Juan Capistrano Library)

Articles

"AIA 1999 Honors and Awards." *Architectural Record* (May 1999), p. 151. (University of Washington, Tacoma Campus Master Plan)

"California Villa." *Architectural Digest* (July 1999), pp. 74–79. (Schetter House)

"Kit of Parts." *House Beautiful* (October 1998), pp. 82–92. (House for the Next Millennium)

"By the Book." *Architecture* (March 1997).

Steele, James (ed.). *Theatre Builders.* London: Academy Editions, 1996. (California Center for the Arts, Escondido)

"The AD 100." *Architectural Digest* (September 1995).

California Gardens. Clarkson N. Potter, 1995. (Yudell/Beebe House)

"Hail to the Haas." *San Jose Mercury News* (May 7, 1995). (Haas School of Business)

"A Last Act: Taking Whimsy to School." *The New York Times* (November 26, 1995). (Haas School of Business)

Ojeda, Oscar Riera. *The New American House.* New York: Whitney Library of Design, 1995. (Yudell/Beebe House)

"Arts Fusion." *Architecture* (December 1994). (California Center for the Arts, Escondido)

"Building for the Arts." *Architecture* (December 1994).

"Moore Ruble Yudell, A Firm on the Go." *The World & I* (July 1994).

School Design. New York: Van Nostrand Reinhold, 1994. (University of Oregon Science Complex)

Steele, James (ed.). *Museum Builders.* London: Academy Editions, 1994. (Hollywood Museum; Renovations to the West Wing of St. Louis Art Museum)

Toy, Maggie (ed.). *World Cities: Los Angeles.* London: Academy Editions, 1994. (Various projects)

Webb, Michael. *Architects House Themselves: Breaking New Ground.* Foreword by J. Carter Brown. The Preservation Press, 1994. (Yudell/Beebe House)

"Designers of the Year." *Interiors* (January 1992). (Nativity Catholic Church)

"Earthly Delights: A California Design Couple's Country Idyll." *House Beautiful* (August 1992), cover.

"Nishiokamoto Housing." *Architecture* (January/February 1992).

"Outdoor Rooms." *Elle Decor* (April/May 1992), cover.

"University of Oregon Science Complex." *Architecture* (March/April 1992).

"1991–1992 Western Home Awards, Award of Merit." *Sunset Magazine* (October 1991), cover.

"Bel Air Presbyterian Church." *American Organist* (February 1991), cover.

"Collaborative Genius," "Angeleno Gothic," "Campus Medicine." *Architecture* (March 1991)

"Feature Story: The Custom Collection." *Builder* (June 1991), cover.

"Humboldt Bibliotek" *American Libraries* (April 1991), cover.

"Malibu on their Minds." *House and Garden* (February 1991), cover.

"Nativity Catholic Church." *Architectural Record* (February 1991), cover.

"Tegel Harbor Housing." *Architecture* (May/June 1991).

"University of Oregon Science Complex." *Architectural Record* (November 1991), cover.

"University of Oregon Science Complex." *Places* (vol. 7, no. 4, 1991), cover.

"Moore Ruble Yudell: A Malibu Residence." *Architectural Digest* (February 1990). (House on Point Dume)

"Pride of Place." *Architectural Record* (January 1990). (Humboldt Library)

The Backyard Book. Viking Penguin, 1988. (King Studio)

"Berlino 1988." *Abitare* (Milan, Italy, May 1988). (Tegel Harbor)

"Housing That's Changing the Face of West Berlin." *The New York Times* (April 14, 1988). (Tegel Harbor)

"Waterfront Housing at Once Exuberant and Classical." *Architecture* (May 1988). (Tegel Harbor Housing)

"Charles Moore." *Interiors* (September 1987), cover. (St. Matthew's Episcopal Church; Church of the Nativity; Humboldt Library)

"Das Pathos endet an der Haustür." *Der Spiegel* (June 1, 1987). (Tegel Harbor Housing)

Langdon, Philip. *American Houses*. New York: Stewart, Tabori & Chang, 1987. (King Studio; Marine Street Residence)

"Living by the Water." *Progressive Architecture* (October 1987), cover. (Tegel Harbor Housing)

"Moore Ruble Yudell: Remodeling a Spanish Colonial House in Beverly Hills." *Architectural Digest* (September 1987), cover. (Pynoos House)

"Perfection in Miniature." *House Beautiful* (February 1987). (King Studio)

"Rebuilding Berlin Yet Again." *Time* (June 15, 1987). (Tegel Harbor Housing)

"Overview of Recent Works." *Space Design* (November 1986). (Tegel Harbor; Plaza Las Fuentes; The Parador Hotel; St. Matthew's Episcopal Church; San Antonio Art Institute; Kwee House)

Street-Porter, Tim. *Freestyle*. New York: Stewart, Tabori & Chang, 1986. (Rodes House; Marine Street Residence)

"Architecture Moore Ruble Yudell." *Architectural Digest* (August 1985). (Kwee House)

"Built on Religious, Regional Tradition: St. Matthew's Church." *Architecture* (May 1984).

"Design by Congregation." *Architectural Record* (February 1984). (St. Matthew's Episcopal Church)

"St. Matthew's Parish Church." *Architecture + Urbanism* (Tokyo, January 1984).

"A Church is Not a Home." *Newsweek* (March 1983). (St. Matthew's Episcopal Church)

"Back to the Classics." *Newsweek* (September 1981). (Rodes House)

"Charles Moore and Company." *Global Architecture* (Tokyo, no. 7, 1981).

"Charles Moore: Recent Projects." *Architectural Review* (London, August 1981).

Erste Projekte. Internationale Bauausstellung Berlin 1984, West Berlin, 1981. (Tegel Harbor)

"Houses of the Year." *Architectural Record* (May 1981). (Rodes House)

"New American Architecture 1981." *Architecture + Urbanis* (Tokyo, 1981).

"Palladio Lives On." *Life Magazine* (New York, 1980). (Rodes House)

Project Credits

Tegel Harbor Master Plan, Housing and Library

Area: 11 hectares

Size of project: 170 units of housing, 200,000 square feet mixed use

Client: Beta Siebente

Competition: 1980

Completion: 1989

Principal architects: Charles Moore, John Ruble, Buzz Yudell

Project architect: Thomas Nagel

Project team: Leon Glodt, Mel Lawrence, Eileen Liebman, Regina Pizzinini, Peter Zingg, Renzo Zechetto

Associate architects: Händel, Wolf und Zell (housing); Abeln, Lubic, Skoda (library)

Consulting architect: Walter Hötzel (library)

Landscape architect: Müller Knippschild Wehberg

Color and materials: Tina Beebe

Peek & Cloppenburg Department Store

Area: 80,000 square feet (retail)

Client: Peek & Cloppenburg GmbH

Competition: 1992

Principal architects: John Ruble, Charles Moore, Buzz Yudell

Project architect: James Mary O'Connor

Project team: Craig Currie, Don Dimster, Chris Duncan, Mark Peacor, John Taft, Curtis Woodhouse, Cecily Young

Bolle Center

Area: 200,000 square feet (office)

Competition: 1990

Principal architects: John Ruble, Buzz Yudell

Project architect: Daniel Garness

Project team: John Davis, Sylvia Deily, Chris Duncan, Arlette Gordon, Mark Peacor, Tea Sapo, John Taft, Mario Violich, Curtis Woodhouse

Friedrichstadt Passagen

Area: 200,000 square feet (retail and offices)

Client: Dumas West & Company, Brian Garrison

Competition: 1991

Principal architects: John Ruble, Buzz Yudell

Project architect: Cecily Young

Project team: John Davis, Chris Duncan, Arlette Gordon, Doug Jamieson, Keri Hogan, Ying-Chao Kuo, Anthony Tam, Tony Tran, Curtis Woodhouse

Associate architects: Frank Williams & Associates, Frank Williams, Frank Uellendahl

Berliner Strasse Housing

Area: 1 hectare

Size of project: 98 luxury condominiums

Client: Groth + Graalfs Industrie und Wohnbau GmbH

Design: 1991–1995

Completion: 1998 (Phase 1)

Principal architects: John Ruble, Charles

Moore, Buzz Yudell

Project architect: Daniel Garness

Project team: Roger Carvalheiro, Craig Currie, Don Dimster, Mary Beth Elliott, Mark Peacor, Marc Schoeplein, John Taft, Curtis Woodhouse

Associate architects: Pysall Stahrenberg & Partner, Ferdinand + Gerth

Landscape architect: Müller Knippschild Wehberg

Color and materials: Tina Beebe

Project liaison: Miller Stevens

Kirchsteigfeld Master Plan and Housing

Area: 53 hectares

Size of project: 2,500–3,000 housing units plus 160,000 square meters of commercial, service, and industrial spaces

Client: Groth + Graalfs Industrie und Wohnbau GmbH

Competition: 1992

Completion: 1997

Principal architects: John Ruble, Buzz Yudell

Competition project architect: Mark Peacor

Competition team: Craig Currie, Richard Destin, Don Dimster, John Taft, Tony Tran, Mario Violich, Celina Welch, Curtis Woodhouse, Cecily Young

Size of project: 160 units of subsidized housing

Housing project architect: Shuji Kurokawa

Housing team: Robert Anderson, Louis Bretana, Mary Beth Elliott, James Mary O'Connor, Steve Gardner, Daniel Garness,

Adrian Koffka, Adam Padua, Mario Violich

Project liaison: Miller Stevens

Associate architect: Lunetto & Fischer
Architekten

Landscape architect: Müller Knippschild
Wehberg

Color and materials: Tina Beebe

Karow Nord

Area: 98 hectares

Size of project: 5,000 housing units, 20,000
square meters of mixed-use and 180,000
square meters of institutional spaces

Client: Groth + Graalfs Industrie und
Wohnbau GmbH

Competition: 1992

Completion: 1999

Principal architects: Buzz Yudell, John Ruble

Master plan project architect: Daniel
Garness

Project coordination: Miller Stevens

Project team: Etchika Badzies, Louis Bretana,
Craig Currie, Mary Beth Elliott, Mark Grand,
Eric Hammerlund, John Johnson, Wing-Hon
Ng, Adam Padua, Mark Peacor, Niels
Turnbull, George Venini, Mario Violich,
Celina Welch, Curtis Woodhouse

Landscape planners: Müller Knippschild
Wehberg

Regional planners: Freie Planungsgruppe
Berlin: Gerard Schneider, Susanne Klar;
Bebauungsplan: Büro Obermeyer, J.
Hoffmann

Renderers: Al Forster, Daniel Garness

Size of project: 100 units of housing

Housing project architect: Daniel Garness

Project team: Robert Anderson, Adrian
Koffka, Shuji Kurokawa, Adam Padua, Mark
Peacor

Associate architect: Lunetto & Fischer
Architekten

Color and materials: Tina Beebe

Size of project: 75 units of housing, 6,000
square meters of retail and office

Town center principal architects: John
Ruble, Buzz Yudell

Town center project architects: Daniel
Garness, Adrian Koffka, Adam Padua

Project team: Robert Anderson, Richard
Destin, Timothy Eng, Mark Grand

Associate architect (Blocks 13, 19 & 22):
Lunetto & Fischer Architekten

Associate architect (Block 15): Ferdinand +
Gerth

Landscape architect: Müller Knippschild
Wehberg

Tiergarten Dreieck Housing and Office

Size of project: 20 luxury condominiums,
health club, 8,000 square meters of office

Client: Groth + Graalfs Industrie und
Wohnbau GmbH

Design: 1996–1997

Completion: 1999

Principal architects: John Ruble, Buzz Yudell

Project architect: Adrian Koffka

Project team: Christian Daniels, Mark
Grand, Christopher Hamilton, Errin
Hillhouse, Adam Padua

Associate architect: Lunetto & Fischer
Architekten

Landscape architect: Müller Knippschild
Wehberg

United States Embassy

Area: 180,000 square feet

Client: United States Department of State

Competition: 1995

Architects: Moore Ruble Yudell with Gruen
Associates

Principal architects (MRY): John Ruble, Buzz
Yudell

Principal architects (Gruen): Jay Booth,
Debra Gerod

Project architect: Cecily Young

Project team: Richard Destin, Adrian Koffka,
Marc Schoeplein, Will Sheppird, Gene
Treadwell

Interiors/space plan: Brayton & Hughes
Design Studio

Environmental/sustainable design: Flack &
Kurtz Consulting Engineers

Structural & blast: Weidlinger Associates,
Inc.

Security & telecommunications: Jaycor

Landscape architect: The Olin Partnership

Color and materials: Tina Beebe

Graphics: Sussman/Prezja & Company, Inc.

Geotech/civil: Mueser Rutledge Consulting
Engineers

Contact architect: Pysall Stahrenberg +
Partner

Renderings: Doug Jamieson

Acknowledgments

Throughout our career in Berlin we have been extraordinarily fortunate in our associations with clients, city officials, and colleagues, many of whom have become life-long friends. In Reinickendorf, where it all began with Tegel Harbor, our developer client Dietmar Otremba proved a dedicated ally in fully realizing an architectural vision, as did City Planning Director Werner Weber, who has given us so much support over the years.

Since Tegel our principal work in Berlin has been with Groth + Graalfs; to Dieter Graalfs, who first invited us, as well as partners Klaus Groth and Gerd Unger, we are deeply grateful for the extraordinary trust and encouragement they have given us. Our ten-year collaboration has provided us with an ongoing opportunity to learn about architecture and urbanism in Berlin, and to apply what we have learned in a series of fascinating and challenging projects. We have truly shared a moment in history together.

Our delightful association with Hartmut Krämer of Peek & Cloppenburg began in Berlin, but was ultimately consummated in Leipzig. Similarly, other clients outside the city, such as Klaus Hoffmann of the Gesellschaft Wirtschaftsförderung Göttingen, have been an important support group to our work in Berlin.

All of our built work in Berlin has been graced by the landscape design of Cornelia Müller and Jan Wehberg. With Zen-like refinement and insight they have produced a series of works which stand on their own, each one relevant and sympathetic to the architectural objectives of our own work, yet unmistakably a part of their broad and splendid contribution to the city.

In much the same way, Tina Beebe's work in color and material design traces her own distinct and parallel career through each of our Berlin projects. What emerges is an overlay, a weave of architectural and visual ideas, from the highly particular composition for Tegel Harbor to the broad color planning of Karow Nord.

Much of the pleasure of working in Berlin has come from some wonderful associations with other architects: with Walter Hoetzel, Alexander Lubic, and Theo Abeln on the Humboldt Library; more recently with planner Miller Stevens on Kirchsteigfeld and Karow Nord; and in continuing collaboration with Eva Lunetto and Jörg Fischer, who have been responsible for the production of most of our built work in Berlin since Tegel Harbor. Their passion, dedication and insight have carried us through extraordinary challenges.

Our collaboration with Rob Krier and Christoph Kohl on Kirchsteigfeld has been profound, helping us to define and evolve our own vision as urban designers on Karow Nord. The two districts may best be understood as sister-cities. On both we were fortunate to have the professional support of Gerhard Schneider and Susi Klar of the Freie Planungsgruppe Berlin, who held us all to high standards of social and physical planning. We have also enjoyed the support and encouragement of Jochen and Anette Grundei of Pysall Stahrenberg + Partner, who have at various stages worked with us on Berliner Strasse and the U.S. Embassy.

Our involvement in Berlin may indeed never have happened but for the early support of Heinrich Klotz, who championed our competition proposal for Tegel Harbor and provided major exhibitions of our work at the Deutsche Architektur Museum. We are grateful to Josef Kleihues for his support, and for the dedicated assistance of Walter Stepp, the late Arnulf Scherer, and many others at the Internationale Bauausstellung Berlin '84, who helped us to realize the work at Tegel Harbor.

For the extraordinary opportunity to present this publication of our Berlin experience we are deeply grateful to Paul Latham and Alessina Brooks at The Images Publishing Group, and graphic designer Rod Gilbert at The Graphic Image Studio. They have shown such a keen understanding of the special nature of this monograph and its editorial and graphic quality—we hope this will be the first of many projects together.

For the concept and inception of *Building in Berlin* we are quite indebted to two close friends: Michael Webb, who traveled to Berlin, extensively researched the entire history of our involvement, and authored the core essay; and our associate James O'Connor, who first encouraged us to pursue the project, and has worked closely with Images to produce it.

This is the second volume on our work which has been edited by Wendy Kohn, and she has provided us with ever more inspired direction. Her passion, skill, and vision have reached into every aspect of design and content, and encouraged us to present fresh perspectives on both new and familiar work. In this, we have been aided tremendously by Adrian Koffka, who has offered an inside/outside point of view as editor, contributing author, and graphic designer.

The design and content have been skillfully supported by Ken Kim, who helped design the overall graphic format, and Tony Tran, who worked tirelessly to assemble archival material and to produce the images themselves.

Having wonderful visual material to present has been our great fortune, which we owe to the varied and wonderful vision of photographers Tim Hursley, Werner Hutmacher, and Richard Bryant.

Our collaborative approach to design has been proven by the dedicated and inspired work of our colleagues at Moore Ruble Yudell, whose role in the work in Berlin has been critical: Dan Garness, who has contributed his own essay to *Building in Berlin* and was central to our work in Berliner Strasse, Kirchsteigfeld, and Karow Nord, as was Cecily Young for the Berlin Embassy, and Adam Padua and Adrian Koffka for our buildings at Tiergarten Dreieck. Defining qualities of each of our European projects have come from the special chemistry of personal collaborations with James O'Connor, Mario Violich, Mary Beth Elliott, and Shuji Kurokawa, to name only a few.

Finally, we wish to thank all of our past and present associates and staff for giving their many talents and supporting the spirit of community which we believe has been essential to the creation of our best and most defining work.

John Ruble and Buzz Yudell
Los Angeles, 1999

Photo Credits

Jaime Ardiles–Acre: 198 (Kwee House, a)

Tom Bonner: 206 (San Rafael Student Housing)

Richard Bryant: 29

Mark Darley: 203 (Walrod Residence)

Annette Del Zoppo: 180 (bottom); 181; 182 (bottom); 184 (top); 189 (bottom); 193 (bottom right); 194 (top right, bottom right)

Lars Finnström: 210 (Potatisåkern Housing)

Groth + Graalfs: 163

Stephen Harby: 199 (Bel Air Presbyterian Church)

Timothy Hursley: 11 (2); 28; 30 (bottom); 35 (top); 40 (top); 41; 46 (top and bottom); 47; 172 (4); 198 (Rodes House); 198 (Tegel Harbor Housing); 198 (Tegel Harbor Villa); 198 (Humboldt Bibliothek); 199 (St. Louis Art Museum); 199 (Carousel Park, b); 199 (Inman House); 199 (Plaza Las Fuentes); 200 (University of Oregon Science Complex); 200 (The Peter Boxenbaum Arts Education Center); 200 (UCSD Cellular and Molecular Medicine, East and West Wings); 200 (First Church of Christ, Scientist); 200 (Yudell/Beebe House); 201 (Walter A. Haas School of Business); 201 (Powell Library Renovation and Addition); 201 (California Center for the Arts); 201

(University of Washington Chemistry Building); 202 (Villa Superba); 202 (Schetter House, a); 202 (University of Washington); 203 (Walrod Residence)

Werner Huthmacher: 10 (1); 12 (4); 22–23: 26–27: 30 (top); 32–33; 34; 35 (bottom); 36–37; 40 (bottom); 43; 44–45; 84–85; 86; 88–89; 90; 91; 94–95; 96; 97 (top and bottom); 98; 99; 103 (9, 10); 106–107; 111 (bottom); 114; 115; 116; 117 (top and bottom); 118–119; 122; 123; 130–131; 133; 135; 136–137; 138 (top and bottom); 139; 140; 141 (top and bottom); 142; 144 (top and bottom); 145; 147; 148 (top); 150; 151 (top); 152–153; 154 (top and bottom); 155; 156; 158; 159; 202 (Berliner Strasse Housing); 202 (Kirchsteigfeld Master Plan and Housing)

Adrian Koffka: 202 (Peek & Cloppenburg Department Store)

Jane Lidz: 200 (Anawalt House)

Erhard Pfeiffer: 87; 93; 112–113

Marc Schoeplein: 205 (Shmuger/Hamagami House)

Alex Vertikoff: 199 (San Antonio Art Institute)

All other photography courtesy of Moore Ruble Yudell.